MATERNITY WARD

FINAL FLIGHT OF A WWII LIBERATOR

AND THE DIARY OF HER WAIST-GUNNER, S/SGT WILLIAM J. FAY

Marguerite Madison Aronowitz

Foreword by Major Robert W. Sternfels

To Brian Callaghan with best wishes. Marguerite Madison Aronowitz January 1999

Pine Castle Books
P.O. Box 4397
Prescott AZ 86302-4397

Publisher's Cataloging-in-Publication
(Provided by Quality Books, Inc.)

Aronowitz, Marguerite Madison, 1938-
        Maternity Ward : final flight of a WWII Liberator, and the diary of her waistgunner, S/SGT William J. Fay / Marguerite Madison Aronowitz ; foreword by Robert W. Sternfels. – 1st ed.
        p.   cm.
        Includes bibliographical references and index.
        Preassigned LCCN: 98-91721
        ISBN: 0-9666615-0-8

        1. B-24 bomber. 2. Fay, William J.—Diaries. 3. World War, 1939-1945—Aerial operations, American. 4. World War, 1939-1945—Personal narratives, American. I. Title.

D790.A76 1998   940.54'49'73
                                 QBI98-1304

Published by: Pine Castle Books
               P.O. Box 4397
               Prescott, AZ 86302-4397

Cover: National Archives Still Pictures

Printed in the United States of America

INTRODUCTION AND DEDICATION

Staff Sergeant William J. Fay, a B-24 gunner, was my cousin. At 22 years of age, he was downed and reported missing in action on August 1, 1943, the day of the famous U.S. Army Air Forces raid on the oil fields of Ploesti, Romania. His B-24, **Maternity Ward**, was forced to ditch in the Ionian Sea after taking severe enemy fire.

Bill's diary was recently discovered among his sister's belongings, along with numerous photos. Several crew members of the 98th Bomb Group have been located by the author, including the pilot of **Maternity Ward**, John V. Ward, who heroically brought the plane to a forced water landing in a desperate attempt to salvage what he could of the plane and its crew.

I was just five years old when our family received a telegram regarding Bill's fate, and I can still remember the handsome soldier who visited us when he was home on furlough. It is to Bill Fay; Captain John V. Ward and the brave crew of **Maternity Ward**; Bill's fellow crew members on **Lil Joe** and **Li'l De-Icer**, especially Captain Wes Egan, T/Sgt John Matheson, and S/Sgt Michael German; and all members of the 98th Bomb Group, both living and dead, that I dedicate this book.

Marguerite Madison Aronowitz
September 1998

iii

Bill Fay, Cairo, February 1943

FOREWORD

Maternity Ward, a pink-colored B-24D piloted by 2/Lt. John V. Ward, was in #3 position, left wing on Major Hahn's plane while I was flying right wing #2 position on our August 1, 1943 low-level mission to the Ploesti Oilfields. Major Hahn was the CO of the 345th Squadron, leading the squadron toward the inferno that awaited us at the assigned Astra Romana Refinery, White IV, designated target for the 98th Bomb Group.

Anyone who has even remotely heard of the North Africa desert campaign, was part of the military operation, or is curious regarding the famous Ploesti low-level raid, should enjoy this book. Living conditions as portrayed in Fay's diary are an accurate accounting of the misery and unbelievable existence we all endured in the hot and dusty Libyan desert of North Africa. How the men of the 98th Bomb Group struggled to keep alive under the most inhumane conditions and still complete as many as 50 missions is recounted here by the talented authoress, Marguerite Madison Aronowitz.

Prior to the Ploesti mission, S/Sgt Bill Fay noted in his diary on June 1 that I helped test hop a plane. This is the only encounter I had with Fay.

> Major Robert W. Sternfels
> Squadron Commander, 345th Squadron,
> 98th Bomb Group
> Pilot of B-24D **Sandman**

TABLE OF CONTENTS

LIST OF PHOTOGRAPHS

LIST OF ILLUSTRATIONS

1. JANUARY 1943

CHOOSING THE RIGHT TIME FOR A LOW-LEVEL ATTACK

Early in 1943, U.S. Army Air Forces teams parachuted into the snow-covered mountains of Yugoslavia to set up observation posts. This was done in order to assess weather conditions leading up to a planned Ploesti (Romania) strike later in the year. Meteorology was critical to military planning. The success or failure of a long-distance flight from North Africa to Romania over heavily defended enemy territory could easily depend on weather conditions.

The chosen aircraft, bomb-laden B-24s, would have no fighter escort, so cloud cover would offer a big advantage until they arrived at the target, where clear skies would be needed. Cloudless skies over Ploesti was the exception, not the rule. In fact, it was and still is known as "the rainy city." Winds were also important. Strong headwinds coming or going would mean not having enough fuel to get back. Southerly winds at the target would spread the American-set *incendiary* fires after the first runs, so the B-24s wouldn't have to bomb more than once.

1

In the months leading up to August 1, 1943, climatologists looked at 40 years of weather maps and surveyed the information gained by their mountain teams. It was determined that the right conditions were most likely to occur in the months of March or August, so August 1, 1943, was chosen. The weather on that day would turn out to be generally favorable, even though towering cloud formations over Albania and Yugoslavia would create serious flying problems for the five participating U.S. bomb groups.

FAY DIARY: January 1, 1943

Here goes, for the first time I am starting to keep one of these bloody diaries. I left the States the 24th of December, 1942. Spent Christmas Eve in Puerto Rico. Took off about 4:00 Christmas Day. Stopped in Georgetown, British Guiana and ate breakfast. Took off around 11:00 am and landed in Belem, Brazil, and spent the rest of the night there. It was not a lovely way to spend Christmas Day.

We then left there on the 26th at about 6:00 am and went to Natal, Brazil. Waited around and then went to Accra, Africa. Spent about 6 to 10 hours there and then took off for Khartoum which was a 2,300-mile non-stop flight. Stayed there overnight and it was a really nice place.

We left early the next morning and landed in Cairo on the 29th. We got our final orders and then came to Fayid. We arrived on the 1st and went around getting ourselves established.

January 2, 1943

Waiting for our first mission.

Heading for the great unknown.

LIFE IN THE DESERT

Sand, relentless sun and heat, and crawling things. Life in the desert in early 1943 was no picnic, but it was a lot better than that being suffered by many troops in the European and Pacific theaters. The days were often boring, but more often than not briefings were held and missions scheduled. The Allied powers were ready to go after enemy forces in Italy and Greece, while in North Africa Rommel's troops were beating a hasty retreat. Waiting for their chance to see some action, B-24 flight crews spent their days on routine assignments and struggling against the elements.

In some base camps, the scenario was often bleak--30 or more B-24s scattered around a runway that was only a strip of dirt scratched in the desert. Besides the mess tent, the location included officers' and enlisted men's tents filled with cots and the bare necessities of life.

The mess tent was usually the focal point of daily life. Spartan as it was, meal time was an important part of each day. Chow in camp was mostly canned rations, consisting of powdered eggs and potatoes, dried beef, hash and *Spam*. Most of the men vowed never to eat another piece of Spam as long as they lived, no matter how it was prepared. Others still like it to this day. Cans of cheese were deemed acceptable and the beans weren't too bad. Some crew members tried to intercept incoming C-ration shipments in order to lay hold of as many beans as they could. Since the cans were small, they could be warmed up on a B-24's engine heater for a snack. Then there was what was charitably referred to as "desert butter," a yellow concoction that wouldn't melt no matter how hot the day. Bread was considered a real treat when it was baked fresh in camp. Blowing sand neutralized most everything that was edible, however. It coated food being carried back to the enlisted men's tents or eaten out in the open. Officers fared better, since they usually ate in the mess tents. Water was trucked in from nearby wells and hung in rubberized *lister bags* after being laced with chlorine. It was used for washing and rinsing eating utensils, shaving, and personal washing.

It wasn't uncommon for the temperature to hit 125°F. Anything metal was too hot to touch. The never-ending sand made its way into every crack and crevice. Nothing stayed dirt-free, and everything mechanical had to be continually taken apart and cleaned. The only escape from soaring temperatures was to get to the Mediterranean for a swim, or wait until nightfall. Flights to higher altitudes brought welcome relief if one could catch an outgoing B-24. In fact, men would sometimes take a plane up for a supposed test run just to cool themselves and refrigerate their beer. The coveted drink could also be cooled by dipping the cans in high octane fuel. When they were taken out the evaporation process acted like a refrigerant. On the other end of the desert weather spectrum, rain turned the sand into a sea of mud that acted like quicksand. Many a plane had to have its wheels dug out, and boots were usually a sorry sight.

For entertainment, movies were shown almost every night, and occasionally a live band and entertainers were brought in to try to take the troops' minds off their plight for a few hours. Poker was a popular pastime, along with reading (if you were lucky enough to have book). Letter writing and mail were high on everyone's list. Pilots looking for something exciting to do would take a B-24 up for a test flight and buzz the *faloukas* on the Nile, knocking them over with prop wash. They also enjoyed buzzing tents.

For all-around everyday annoyance there were flies that never quit and an assortment of locusts and grasshoppers that infiltrated even the tightest netting. Locusts with wing spans of 6-8" were known to completely cover everything and everyone for days on end. Rats and mice nested anywhere they pleased and desert scorpions crawled into clothes and bedding. Heat, blowing sand, bugs and Spam paint a pretty fair picture of life in the desert as experienced by members of the 98th and other bomb groups that had set up housekeeping in the North African desert.

Bill Moffett on washday.

Time out for recreation.

FAY DIARY: January 13, 1943

Today we went on our first mission and the designated spot was Tripoli, but due to a sudden change of wind, a 100-mile-per-hour headwind, it threw us off course and the mission was a failure. We stayed out two hours over schedule with #2 engine leaking gas. We just made it home with only a few gallons of gas to spare. We flew in the plane named **Gump**. [**Gump the Sniffer Dog** was one of the first radar-equipped planes in the 98th.]

January 14, 1943

Feeling low because of our failure on our first mission. Starting to look forward to some mail.

January 17, 1943

Target once again Tripoli--merchant vessels and warehouses. Flew to Post 159 in the ship named **Pluto**, and refueled. Got further information on targets, weather, wind, etc. Stayed overnight.

January 18, 1943

Carrying five one-thousand-pound bombs. We flew at 26,000 feet. *Ack-ack* pretty accurate--hit our plane and knocked #3 engine out of whack. Rear turret hit by ack-ack but only part of the glass broke and did not injure [Charles] Jarboe. Saw buildings fly apart and one or two vessels burning in the harbor.

Going away from the target we were attacked by six German planes--five *ME-109s* and one *Stuka*. They hit one plane out of nine but did not knock it down. It was damn cold up there and my fingers were numb. On the way back Jarboe passed out due to lack of oxygen. Finally got back to our base around midnight.

Charles Jarboe.

January 19, 1943

Didn't get up 'till noon and went to chow. Went into town and to a show titled "Shylock." Came back to camp and hit the hay and started to dream of a certain _day when I'd meet up with a certain lass back home.

January 20, 1943

Waiting for another assignment. Played blackjack and won about a Pound, which is about $4.12 in American greenbacks. Should be due for another mission soon, and the sooner the better as I'll be able to get home sooner.

January 21, 1943

Flew this morning. Practiced interphone and fire direction, also a few landings and take-offs.

January 22, 1943

Tripoli should fall today for sure. Due to our blitz air attack and also Allied ground troops moving into Tripoli. The Germans are evacuating.

January 23, 1943

Confirmed reports came that Tripoli fell at sunrise this morning. I also received my first mail over here. One from Betty.

January 24, 1943

Went to church today and met Capt. Raphel. He said he's headed back to the U.S. with his crew.

Still waiting for our plane to have an engine change. The plane we are getting has over 500 hours (combat), and also new engines. It has a few holes, but they're patched up and it also has 30 missions and two German planes to its credit. Here's hoping it holds up for another 500 hours.

January 25, 1943

The plane is still not ready to fly. Perhaps Tripoli will be our next base, or damn close to it.

January 26, 1943

Our plane was ready today and was taken up for a test flight and all the engines performed okay. Tomorrow probably the ship will be taken to high altitude for tests and then we will resume our missions. Well, another day passes and a day closer to getting home.

January 27, 1943

We test hopped the plane again this morning and shot around 2,000 rounds of ammunition. This afternoon the plane was taken to about 26,000 feet and everything seems to be okay, so we should be due for another mission.

January 28, 1943

Today we went out and cleaned our guns on the ship. This afternoon the pilot, co-pilot, and engineer and radio man took a load of bombs to *L.G.159*.

January 29, 1943

We started to take off but a sandstorm was blowing at about 35 to 45 miles per hour. We did however take off at 2:00 pm and arrived at L.G.140 at 5:30 and got our test and went to bed. This is really a rugged place.

January 30, 1943

Got up and ate breakfast, and if we eat much more of this food we'll all have the shits. Very damp and also only about 180 miles from Crete.

Our take-off was at 1:00 right after dinner, with our target being Messina, Sicily. We went along fine until #1 engine started to smoke. We tried to gain altitude anyway, but then the #3 engine prop governor went flooey and so we had to come back. We were trying to get over the target ourselves and it's lucky we didn't, as a number of ME-109s were waiting for us. Landed back here about 10:00 pm and it took about two hours to find our tent in this lovely desert. We flew in the B-24 **Li'l De-Icer**.

January 31, 1943

Lovely day, windy as hell and chilly. I don't know when our plane will be ready for another mission. Well, this really is a swell place. No water, and very little food. Trucks and everything scattered around here. I don't know when I'll get a chance to wash as water is needed for drinking. Looks like Arizona. There are six of us sleeping in a tent and the cots are so close to each other that we almost fall over on one another.

2. FEBRUARY 1943

THE B-24

The boxcar. An aluminum cigar. Pink elephants. No matter what they called the B-24 Liberator, it was a formidable weapon against the enemy in World War II, and a worthy ship of the desert.

This famous bomber came in different colors and featured varied armaments depending on the year of production and which company built it. Approximately 19,000 planes were produced between 1939 and 1945 by Consolidated Vultee (San Diego and Fort Worth), Douglas Aircraft (Tulsa), Ford Motor Company (Willow Run), and North American Aircraft (Dallas). **Maternity Ward**, a B-24D, was built by Consolidated San Diego. To help it blend in with the environment, she was painted a "desert sand" color, otherwise known as sand-pink.

The B-24, a 10-man-crew ship, weighed more than 60,000 pounds when fully loaded. It was designed to carry a pilot, co-pilot, navigator, bombardier, radio operator, flight engineer, and four gunners (top turret, rear, right waist and left waist). Built with light-weight materials to carry maximum bombs, fuel, guns and ammunition, its aluminum skin was thin enough to be

11

cut with a knife. It had four Pratt & Whitney 1200 HP engines, carried 2,750 gallons of fuel, and featured the high-lift, low-drag Davis wing. Most versions had ten 0.5 inch (50 caliber) Browning machine guns and carried either ten 500-lb bombs or five 1,000-lb bombs. The machine guns provided an almost complete field of defensive fire that was often deadly to enemy fighter pilots, especially when they tried attacking several B-24s flying close together. The B-24's range was up to 2,850 miles with a maximum speed of 303 mph, and it could fly as high as 32,000 feet. Typically the Liberator flew high-altitude missions of 18,000 to 28,000 feet, but the famous low-level 1943 Ploesti raid had pilots skimming along at tree-top level.

Unlike today's planes, B-24s were neither pressurized nor heated. Flight crews wore sheepskin-lined leather jackets, helmets and mitts. Not until after the Ploesti mission were crew members issued *flak* jackets and metal helmets. Heavy clothing was therefore often the only barrier between life and a piece of lethal *shrapnel*. At high altitudes, where temperatures could reach -30°F or colder, oxygen masks often froze to the wearer's face. When saliva turned to ice, it blocked the oxygen tube, resulting in the crew member passing out. Touching machine guns with bare hands was also extremely hazardous, as it resulted in skin freezing and attaching itself to the metal.

B-24s also had no windshield wipers, so when flying in the rain pilots sometimes had to stick their heads out the side window to look for critical landmarks, especially runways and landing lights. Afternoon desert landings were also tricky because high winds could whip the dust up several thousand feet into the air.

Pilots did not like to ditch the Liberator in the water because of its high wings and soft underbelly. Other problems were gas leaks and fumes, and lack of response time.

Regardless of its shortcomings, however, the B-24 was a long-range bomber that took incredible punishment and stayed aloft. It was long-range, fast, maneuverable and rugged, and was famous for its ability to strike its blow and return to base under the greatest of handicaps.

During combat, many of these multi-use Liberators were shot out of the sky, but many more limped back to base truly on a wing and a prayer. Some had two engines shot out, hundreds of holes in the wings and fuselage, or fuel tanks punctured, and yet they flew. Some belly-flopped in corn fields or skidded down runways with no landing gear in place. Others, with their nose wheel stuck, survived the landing but finished their run with the nose to the ground and the tail sticking up in the air.

It's no wonder that the B-24 holds an honored place in aviation history as one of the most widely used and depended-upon U.S. aircraft in World War II. It may forever remain behind the sleek B-17 "Flying Fortress" in the public image, but the B-24's role as a trusty "home-away-from-home" to thousands of young flight crews during World War II makes it a very special plane indeed.

After the war most of the battle-weary planes were retired and eventually scrapped. With the post-war demand for aluminum, many wound up being melted down and refashioned into pots and pans, among other things. As of today, only one combat B-24 is known to be flying. The fully restored **All American** (formerly **Golden Girl**) spends 10 months of the year touring the United States thanks to the Collings

Foundation of Stow, Massachusetts. Ten more B-24s can be seen in the following locations: Wright Patterson AFB in Dayton, Ohio (**Strawberry Bitch**); Castle Air Museum in Atwater, California (**Shady Lady**); Lackland AFB in San Antonio, Texas (Ser. No. 44-51228) (will be loaned to the American Air Museum in Duxford, England, sometime in 1999); 8th Air Force Museum in Barksdale, Louisiana (**Laiden Maiden**); Fantasy of Flight Museum in Polk City, Florida; Pima Air and Space Museum in Tucson, Arizona (**Bungay Buckaroo**); Canadian National Aeronautical Museum in Ottawa, Canada; Aerospace Museum in Cosford, England; Indian Air Force Museum in Delhi, India; and one currently being restored in Sidney, Australia.

An RLB30/C-87 cargo transport version of the B-24 named **Diamond Lil** is flown by the Confederate Air Force out of Midland, Texas.

In addition to the above-mentioned Liberators, the wreckage of **Hadley's Harem** was located in 1996 in the waters of the Mediterranean off the coast of Turkey near Antalya by Roy Newton, who flew as gunner on the downed ship, and film-maker Peter Frizzell. It had ditched in the water in a desperate attempt by the pilot to make land after the August 1, 1943, Ploesti raid. The remains of pilot Gilbert Hadley and co-pilot James "Rex" Lindsey were still in the cockpit when it was found.

The plane had broken into three pieces, and only the cockpit was successfully brought up. After the remains of the pilot and co-pilot were returned to the United States for burial with full military honors in 1997, the cockpit was put on display in the Rahmi M. Koç Industrial Museum in Hasköy, Turkey. Newton and Frizzell, along with the owner of the museum, hope to bring the remaining two sections of **Hadley's Harem** to the surface during the summer of 1998.

14

Consolidated's B-24 assembly line in Fort Worth, Texas, during the early 1940s. (The Collings Foundation)

The only combat B-24 still flying: **All American (Golden Girl)** owned the by the Collings Foundation of Stow, Massachusetts. (Collings Foundation)

Bungay Buckaroo, B-24 now housed in the Pima Air and Space Museum, Tucson, Arizona. (Pima Air and Space Museum)

Cockpit of the
All American.

The Collings Foundation
flies a B-24 and B-17 to
over 130 cities each year,
supported entirely by
public donations.
Contributions to this
effort may be sent to the
Collings Foundation, Box
248, Stow, MA 01775.

Inside the fuselage
of **All American**.

B-24 **Li'l De-Icer** in 1943,

all shined up and ready to roll with proud crew
members Byron Chiverton and John Matheson.

Pilot Andrew Opsata's B-24, **Old Blister Butt**, dropping its salvo of 12 bombs over Vegasack, Germany, on October 10, 1943. (Andrew Opsata)

Flight crew (389th) of **Stinger** after flying with the 98th and returning safely from the August 1, 1943 raid on Ploesti.

Standing L-R: radio operator Paul Nicholson; navigator Joe LaLonde; armour gunner John Gormey; co-pilot Louis Quagliano. Kneeling L-R: top turret gunner Jonn Oakes; engineer Charles Quinlan; pilot Andrew Opsata; bombardier Don Discosol. (Andrew Opsata)

Damaged B-24 plows into a field. (National Archives Still Pictures)

Damaged B-24, belly up, goes into a dive. It was hit by the body of an American parachutist who had jumped from a flak-ridden Liberator flying above. The impact took off part of the wing and killed the parachutist. (National Archives Still Pictures)

FAY DIARY: February 1, 1943

We woke up about 9:00 and cooked ourselves a little breakfast in front of our tent as the mess hall is about five miles away. Then we wandered out in the desert and looked at the different things lying around left by Americans, English, Germans, etc. Got paid for the month of January and I collected $130 or 32 Pounds and some piastres. What a place to get paid. Played blackjack tonight and won about 16 Pounds which would be around $70 in greenbacks. What I couldn't do with this dough back home! Here I can't even spend a penny.

February 2, 1943

Plane is ready to fly but all planes are held up because the oil has not reached us yet. We have gas but no oil.

Had a dream last night and dreamt I was home on furlough, so I know it must have been a dream. I met Betty and she said she'd go out with me Saturday night as she wanted to pitch some woo before she got married the next night, Sunday. I don't like that kind of dream. I sure hope it's not a reality until I am there to make it so. I mean for me to be the groom.

February 3, 1943

We ate lunch early, then trucks took us out to our ships. The engines were all warmed up and bombs loaded when the oil pressure dropped and the #1 engine went flooey again. I wanted to go on this one especially as it was a larger one consisting of 38 ships led by Killer Kane. The target was Palermo, Sicily. Well, I guess that's the way things go. Goodnight.

22

February 4, 1943

This afternoon we dug slit trenches for an air attack.

February 5, 1943

The plane is ready for another test hop. I hope it's okay now so we can resume our work. Jarboe and I took a walk out over the desert and found German shoes. We saw a snake and I still don't like those babies. There were some exploding *snaddey bombs*. I didn't pick up anything as there are booby traps around.

Jarboe is really farting tonight as he ate an extra large helping of beans. He's worse than he was last night and that's something. We'll have to move him outside or else we'll have to move. If the enemy possesses the gas Jarboe does we'll be defeated in two months.

February 6, 1943

Yesterday the plane performed okay below 10,000 feet. Today it was taken up to 23,000 feet to make sure the engines are performing okay. Everything is ready for another mission now.

Yesterday [Mike] German, [Bill] Moffett, [Wes] Egan and Gandy [Dave Gandin] broke the ice by receiving mail. It means I should receive some this month for sure, that is if anyone wrote me. Nothing to do so I'm just sitting around the tent and I can hear high-powered explosions at Tobruk, and Tobruk is not over 50 miles from here.

February 7, 1943

Went to church this morning. I obtained a rosary from Father and had a little chat with him. Looks like no mission today. I believe we are going to move to Benghazi pretty soon.

February 8, 1943

I was awakened at 5:30 this morning and told to go get breakfast and that take-off would be at 7:30 am. We took off and our target was Messina, Sicily.

We flew in **Li'l De-Icer**. The ack-ack was really heavy and we had few holes in our right wing. We were attacked by five German planes and I fired about 200 rounds and hit one several times. But the bombardier (Moffett) said he also hit it so we flipped a coin and a I lost so he got credit for it. All the fellows in back knew I really should have received the credit. One plane came right at Jarboe and his guns jammed. He really sweated it out. The plane that fired the most dove right at me and I really poured the lead into him. His plane was really shooting at me and I don't see how he missed, but it's lucky he did cuz I'm still around.

February 9, 1943

Nothing doing today. We went out to our plane and cleaned it up. This afternoon we played catch. Mail was received by some members of our crew, but I have yet to receive some. Good nite, sleep tight, don't let the desert snakes bite.

February 10, 1943

Some of the squadron is starting to move and the

place is Benghazi. Received my first letter today and it was from Al (Madison) and it was really nice.

February 11, 1943

Ready to go on a mission but due to ceiling zero over our target we were grounded.

February 12, 1943

Got hold of a German jacket today, and it's so small I doubt if it would fit Betty. This evening a group of English lads came over to our tent and we told jokes and had fun or what is fun in this part of the country.

February 13, 1943

Mission today, and the target was Naples. We took off at 10:30 and started high altitude at 2:30 and was on oxygen until 7:30. It was about the poorest visibility I've seen so far, a very heavy overcast. However, there was one spot we bombed through. Out of 18 planes four of us reached the target.

Mike [German] was almost done for when his oxygen mask froze and when I was helping him mine froze and I had one hard time trying to get my breath. My feet and hands were frost bitten and they really hurt when they started to thaw out.

A vessel shot at us on the way back. I saw a volcano for the first time, Mt. Vesuvius. There were lots of mountains all full of snow caps. We landed back at 10:00 this evening and the outboard engines went dry. We saw two enemy aircraft but they did not attack us and we were lucky as that was the time we were having oxygen trouble. Also Jarboe's guns froze and Pop's [Byron Chiverton] gummed up and one in the nose also.

February 14, 1943

We packed our things and took off about 2:30 this afternoon for Benghazi which is our next base. However, the runways were muddy and so we had to turn around and come back.

This evening all the crew came to our tent and we chatted until about 11:00. We didn't have any lights because the red alarm was on. It was a beautiful moonlit night but it's only good for raids here.

February 15, 1943

After supper we got a command performance on the radio in our plane. The program featured Bob Burns, Dinah Shore and Tommy Dorsey. The numbers were "He's My Guy," "Song of India," and "We'll Meet Again." It was really nice and makes one feel homesick. Listened to the London News and heard the British Eighth Army is going great while the Americans are being pushed back. The whole crew gathered together tonight in our tent and I pulled out my song sheets and we all sang.

February 16, 1943

During these past few days everyone has really gotten to know one another and their feelings. Both the officers and we enlisted men. We've been getting along pretty good lately and I'd like to see it continue until we're through with this war. Had a lot of fun with Gandy and Moffett the last few days. Gandy and I sang songs together.

We had to pack up and move again today. We got to our new base. It has a few blades of grass. There are about 100 Italian and German planes lying around.

We are about 12 miles from Benghazi. It rains quite often here and at present it's rather muddy.

Nattily attired crew of **Lil Joe**, May 14, 1943

Top L-R: 2/Lt. Wes Egan, pilot; 2/Lt. John Stallings; 2/Lt. David Gandin, navigator; 2/Lt. Bill Moffett, bombardier; 2/Lt. Byron "Pop" Chiverton, engineer/gunner. Bottom L-R: S/Sgt. Bill Fay, waist gunner; S/Sgt. Charles Jarboe, tail gunner; T/Sgt. John Matheson, radio operator and upper turret gunner; S/Sgt. Mike German, waist gunner.

Top: Heinkel HE-111 twin-engine bomber with crew of four
Middle: Similar to Junkers JU 52 tri-motor transport
Bottom: Messerschmitt ME-110 heavy fighter bomber (night
   fighter)

Top: Junkers JU 87 Stuka 2-seat dive bomber
Middle: Messerschmitt ME-109 single-seat fighter
Bottom: Instructions in German regarding oil filter

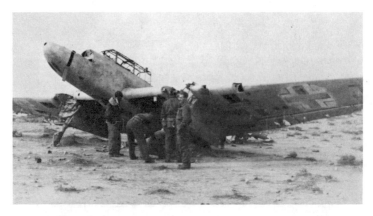

Top: Messerschmitt BF-110 long-range fighter with crew of two or
  three
Middle: Junkers JU 88 bomber
Bottom: Messerschmitt ME-109 single-seat fighter

February 17, 1943

Benina Airdrome is the name of the field at which we are now stationed. We had a basketball game with the English ack-ack boys and played it their way.

About 8:30 pm there was heavy bombing by the Axis a few miles away. You could hear dive bombers. The *pom-pom* and ack-ack looked like a large display of fireworks. While the heaviest bombing was taking place and we were outside of our tent watching, from a tent close by came a tune over the radio. It was "I'm Getting Sentimental Over You."

February 18, 1943

I took off all my clothes and took a bath about 4:00 this afternoon. Felt really swell and like going out on a date, but as far as I could go was around the tent and back, struttin like a kid in his first pair of long pants.

All dressed up with nowhere to go.

February 19, 1943

Got up this morning and first thing two letters were handed to me. My first one was from Betty, and the contents really made me feel swell. There aren't enough words to express my feelings, and lover keeps 'em coming.

They had a show tonight and it was pretty good. Jokes and a few songs. There were three Army nurses there--all over 50 years old.

February 20, 1943

Took off for another mission at 12:30 right after lunch. The target was Naples which is about as hot with ack-ack as Berlin. We stayed on oxygen for 4-1/2 hours. The overcast was very heavy and no enemy aircraft was sighted by us. Four planes, however, ran into some, and three returned. I saw some bombs demolish a little village completely. We landed about 11:00 pm. Just received news that we have a seven-day pass coming up and it starts tomorrow. We're going to Alexandria and I hear it's quite a place.

February 21, 1943

Got up at 6:45 and took off for Alexandria. We buzzed everything along the way and damn near hit a cliff with the belly of the ship. We landed on a field about 30 miles from Alexandria and had to hitchhike in. We took a hot shower and shaved and got a room with a nice soft bed. Went out and raised a little cain.

February 22, 1943

Went shopping and bought some socks, work

clothes, and also a pen and ink as you notice by the green color. Also bought some writing paper and some envelopes. I was kidding with some French gals and they called me "glamour boy."

February 23, 1943

Walked around town. It rained most of the day and was rather chilly. Bought a quart of scotch and found out it was part whiskey, part tea, and mostly water. Here's to another day gone by and one closer to home (I hope).

February 24, 1943

Took in a show this afternoon and then this evening we got powerful drunk and broke glasses on the floor. When we got home I had to carry Jarboe from the elevator to our room.

February 25, 1943

Everyone woke up with a heavy head except me and I can't understand that part of it. We left Alex at noon and arrived in Cairo at 3:45 pm. Some old mail reached me today. I received 21 letters, with six from Betty. I read them over two and three times and I hope she writes me more like that.

February 26, 1943

Visited the Sphinx and the Pyramids. I rode a camel for the first time in my life and it was fun. Went to a picture show then came to a dance they had here for soldiers. I did some dancing, but I sure wish it was Betty I was dancing with.

February 27, 1943

I was so pooped out from what little dancing I did that I slept until almost 11:00. Finally got up and ate and then went and saw "Come Live With Me." Came back and then went out and drank until about 9:30 pm, then took in another show, "Remember the Day." That's the last one I'll see until I get another leave.

February 28, 1943

Took off from Cairo about 1:10 pm. Some really rough flying and we got lost for three hours or more, but then we finally landed okay. Well, here's the end of the second month, and I hope I see a million more of them.

Chiverton, Fay, Jarboe and German in Egypt.

3. MARCH 1943

BENGHAZI AND THE ALLIED FORCES IN NORTH AFRICA

Benghazi, Libya, is located on the northernmost coast of Africa where it is the main seaport. In the 7th Century B.C., Libya was colonized by the Greeks, and by 525 B.C. it was under Egyptian rule. In 96 B.C., the Romans came in and took over. In recent times, Italy established colonies in the 1930s, and by the time World War II began, 18% of the population was Italian. The native North Africans wanted the Italians out, so they supported the British who came in January 1941. Rommel and his Afrika Korps drove out the British in June 1942, and it was a long hard struggle between the Germans and British. Benghazi was the major supply port, and the Germans had three large airfields near Benghazi. Once the British, with the help of the United States, pushed back the Axis forces in North Africa in the fall of 1942, the United States began moving in troops.

Details about the United States' first attempt at invading North Africa are generally not well publicized. *Operation Torch*, as it was called, occurred November 8-

11, 1942, and the enemy turned out to be fighting forces considered to be our allies: the French, including the French Foreign Legion. The situation was complicated by there being three separate French factions controlling Morocco, Algeria and Tunisia. *Operation Torch* was primarily a British and American beach landing made up of 107,000 troops (75% U.S.) who were assigned to capture five ports: three in Morocco and two in Algeria. The French Navy's ships were sitting in the Algiers harbor, and the United States feared they would be scuttled by the French and the harbor made unusable.

As the invasion began, things did not go smoothly. The U.S. 34th Infantry sent landing craft with equipment and 650 men into the port of Algiers where they were supposed to secure the docks. During the effort, jeeps became bogged down in the sand and tanks sunk in the mud. Two British destroyers went into the harbor and were hit by French coastal batteries that were expected to have been neutralized by the invading troops. Fifteen Americans and 9 British onboard were killed, while 33 Americans and 18 British were wounded.

At Oran, Algeria, two Coast Guard cutters were hit while trying to get their commandos into port. This "charge of the 700" resulted in 189 Americans and 113 British being killed. Also, 158 Americans and 86 British were wounded, with survivors being taken as prisoners. The famous 1st Ranger Battalion fared better as they scaled the cliffs near Oran, took out the coastal guns, and captured a Foreign Legion garrison. Farther south, U.S. troops fought with French and African troops as British and French fighters engaged in aerial dogfights.

After flying in from England, paratroopers from the 509th Parachute Infantry Regiment went after two Algerian airfields, not knowing what to expect from the

French. Many of the planes became lost, and paratroopers dropped into Spanish Morocco by mistake were taken prisoner.

Landing craft accidentally dumped troops overboard on the Moroccan coast who had to drop their backpacks and supplies to keep from drowning. American warships tried to knock out coastal batteries all along the coast, including those near Casablanca. It was a tough fight and ironic in that American and British lives were lost to combat with a country that was to be eventually liberated by Allied forces.

When U.S. officers, in an attempt to stop the fighting, finally talked to a French commander under a flag of truce, he said he had no orders to surrender. When General George Patton tried to negotiate a truce after having successfully landing at Casablanca, his emissary was turned away. After General Patton threatened a naval barrage on Casablanca, the French finally surrendered. It took four days of fighting before the United States, Great Britain and France once again became allies. The cost was high. The United States and Great Britain had combined losses of 556 killed-in-action, 837 wounded-in-action, and 41 missing-in-action. France reported corresponding numbers of 700, 1,400 and 400.

As tragic as this invasion appears to be, however, it in fact laid the groundwork for later successful landings in Italy and France. This campaign gave the Allied leaders vital experience with amphibious landings and cemented the American-British war effort. It proved the need for air support in such operations, and demonstrated how maintaining supply lines was vital to winning the war.

Less than two months after *Operation Torch,* five desert-bound bomb groups began moving into North Africa by truck, train and air. By the time Bill Fay and his crew arrived in Fayid, Egypt, on January 1, 1943, they found a well-equipped R.A.F. base where American and British forces were starting to attack Germany's resources in Italy and Greece. Before long, however, the men of the 44th, 93rd, 98th, 376th and 389th packed up and moved to abandoned airfields near Benghazi.

In February 1943, Benina Main and Lete became home to the young men who would make their mark in history by participating in the most famous low-level attack of World War II: the August 1, 1943 raid on the Ploesti oil fields. This large area in North Africa, a huge dust bowl, was a former Italian air base that had changed hands many times. Craters caused by German, Italian, British and American bombs could be seen among the twisted remnants of enemy-built hangars and airdrome installations. Numerous aircraft wrecks and junkyards adorned the landscape.

North Africa, an unlikely battlefield, was terribly scarred by the events of the war and the marauding invaders who came to use it for their own purposes. The once-beautiful city of Benghazi suffered considerably. By 1945, when the war ended, the city and surrounding area was in ruins.

Desert briefing.

Planning a raid on Italy.

So many men, so few knew about Ploesti.

FAY DIARY: March 1, 1943

Well, one day is over in this third month of the year "43" and I hope to get home this fall sometime.

March 2, 1943

Had a briefing for a mission over Messina, but due to bad weather it was called off until tomorrow. I met Dan Farley, a lad I went through gunnery school with. He just came over here to replace a crew that crashed in Turkey.

March 3, 1943

I didn't get up in time for roll call, so if I don't talk fast I may find myself on *K.P.* We had a briefing this morning and they changed the target from Messina to Naples. And that's really a hot target. The last mission over there, one ship was lost and one other was believed to have made it to Malta.

We took off at 12:15 this afternoon and started for Naples. Due to some mistake in navigation by the lead ship we almost went over Greece. In fact, we did touch part of Greece. The rest of the ships turned around and went home but two of us looked around and found some bridges on the east coast of Italy. We bombed them and then came home. Lucky no pursuits came after us as some of our guns were out of order.

March 4, 1943

Beans for supper and so we should have plenty of music tonight.

March 6, 1943

About nine bells this morning Jarboe, Pop [Chiverton] and I went to Benghazi. We hitchhiked about 12 miles. It is really a blown down place although at one time I do believe the town was really picturesque. They have a salvage dump and there's everything imaginable there. It's a junk dealer's dream.

We came back and all the ships were gone and we saw them overhead and thought they were going on a mission and we'd really catch hell. But it proved to be a practice and so everything was okay.

March 7, 1943

Woke up at 7:00 and went to chow. I had one flapjack (or something like one) and a nice cup of cold coffee. This afternoon we went back to Benghazi and the junk yard. I picked up a few rifles and three Italian machine guns. We also picked up parts for about ten motorcycles, but I hope we can make one out of it all. We have another practice mission tomorrow. I believe they're getting ready for something pretty big. I expect them to make Africa another Dunkirk.

March 8, 1943

Another practice mission. Fixed up the three Italian machine guns--I'm going to try to smuggle one home.

March 9, 1943

Another practice mission this morning and I didn't get up in time, so now I suppose Egan will blow his top. Bumped into a lad from Ireland and he said he believes the war will end when the big shots make enough money. Last day of smoking as lent starts tomorrow.

March 10, 1943

Went up on a practice flight and had pursuits-- the real McCoy. We're picking up the Colonel [Kane] and General [Brereton] tomorrow. Received another letter from Betty and also a snapshot.

March 11, 1943

We flew again this morning and had P-40s chasing us again. The Colonel [Kane] and General [Brereton] watched the show.

It's started to rain, so it's one of those days for dreaming. The new crews are in, and those who have 300 hours in are going home.

March 12, 1943

Took a shower and changed clothes. Feel pretty damn good. We tapped a line and I bummed a couple of bulbs from the *Limeys* and so we have electric lights.

March 13, 1943

Stood roll call and then we had a briefing at 10:00. The target again was Naples and we held number three position in the first element. I had two boxes of 150 lbs. each incendiaries. The overcast was really heavy and only once did we get a glimpse of land. Don't know for sure if it was Naples or not. On the way back we ran into a thunderstorm and had to go back up to 23,000 feet. It was really cold!

March 14, 1943

Played volleyball with Moffett, Egan and another Lieutenant. Went out to the plane and listened to an English and a German broadcast. They both contradict each other. They put nine 500-lb bombs on our plane, so we're due for something tomorrow if the weather is good.

March 15, 1943

No mission. Pop brought out two quarts of Canadian Club, so Matheson, Pop and I finished them.

March 16, 1943

About 5:30 this morning I heard someone getting up so I put my flashlight on him and it was Matheson going out to pee and I really had to go myself. I followed Math out and the dog that was sleeping in our tent followed me out. Math stopped and started to empty his bladder and so I stopped right next to him and did likewise. The dog pulled alongside of me and he started, then the three of us marched back into the tent.

Sent Bunge a money order so he can buy Betty some flowers.

March 17, 1943

Sober today, but I'll make up for it this coming New Year's Eve.

Heading to a briefing. (Center: K.K. Phillips;
right: Mike German)

Getting her in top shape.

March 18, 1943

It was raining most of the day but a mission was scheduled. One flight of planes took off at 2:00 this afternoon, and we were supposed to take off at 8:00 this evening. The first planes were supposed to go over and start fires, then we would bomb about midnight. We were called off, and on the way taxiing back our nose wheel sheared off and the bombs flew all over. It was just a prayer that helped us from being blown to bits. On one of the bombs the whole safety device was gone, and all it needed was a little jar to blow. Pop and I finally walked back in mud up to our knees.

March 19, 1943

I believe we're going to lose our ship, **Li'l De-Icer**. The nose wheel braces are all snapped and the bombay doors gone.

Pop finally shot the mouse that was running around our tent. I spotted some new mice that have taken over where old Herb left off. I hope it starts clearing up so we can get in some combat time.

March 20, 1943

Something happened today that wasn't very damn nice. A civil employee of Douglas Aircraft [Pop Reynolds] was killed when our plane's nose wheel gave way and the ship fell on him.

FAY DIARY: March 21, 1943

After chow I went to church and then came back
and straightened out our tent. Another field mouse
popped up and I shot him; now Pop (Chiverton) and I
each have one to our credit.

March 22, 1943

Buried Mr. Fieldmouse today and had a two-gun
burial. We sat around and gabbed and told tales of
back home and what we're going to do when we get
back.

March 23, 1943

Had waffles this morning and then stood roll call.
All were informed of Max's death. Also Burky and
Hutch are in pretty bad shape. Watched some British
Hurricanes buzz the field. Went to mass, where I went
to confession and communion. It's the first time since
June of '42. The news this evening is pretty good. The
Americans and British are both gaining on Tunisia.

March 24, 1943

Had a briefing at 9:00 am, and the target was Messina. We took off at 11:30 am and reached our target about 3:00. We were under ack-ack for about 70 minutes. One gun was all that worked. Five planes attacked us but none were knocked down. They dropped bombs on us from above and almost hit us. We had an oil leak in number 2 engine, but it was all right.

Pop [Chiverton] and I took the tunnel gun out and tried to shoot it by sticking it out my waist window. We tested the flaps and landing gear before we got to the field, and Gandin and Moffett's baggage was on the nose wheel door and it fell out and landed in a little village. We flew in the plane **Lil Joe**, and I believe it's going to be our plane from now on.

EXCERPT FROM DAVID GANDIN'S DIARY, March 31, 1943:

"Today, Captain Vandegraft and we (sic) recommended Fay and Chiv•ton for a Silver Star medal for their outstanding work on the last mission. It was no easy task to fire a tunnel machine gun from the waist window without getting almost thrown out of the airplane. There's little doubt that their action kept pursuit from getting too confident and from coming in close for the kill when most of our guns were out. They're fine boys and deserve some recognition and appreciation of their work."

FAY DIARY: March 25, 1943

Had morning chow—one cup of coffee and one slice of that delicious Spam. We went out to the ship while the Beaver, Inc. [Wes Egan] went to get the bag that fell out of the plane. Here's hoping I get some mail tomorrow.

Woke up and ate then started to tear down the tent. Then we loaded **Lil Joe** and it was time for dinner. We took off right after lunch and landed at Berka No. 2 a few miles southwest of Benghazi. Our plane is about two miles from our tent and our tent is about a block from the Mediterranean. We went for a swim.

March 27, 1943

Built ourselves a fire and heated up some rations. Then we built a crapper and it was time for dinner. After we ate we picked up a German motorcycle on the way back to the tent. Pop started to fix it up. Charlie [Jarboe] and I walked along the beach to Benghazi, which is about four to five miles. The sea is really beautiful, like what one sees in the travel talkies. When we got back I had one letter from Betty. Fourteen boys from our squadron are going home tomorrow.

March 28, 1943

Laid in the sun and took a dip. Also fixed up my Italian machine gun.

March 29, 1943

Stood in line to get my one bottle of beer for the week. Listened to the news and it seems they have Rommel on the run.

48

March 30, 1943

After dinner Pop [Chiverton], Charlie and I put that old German engine together and I do believe it will work. We wrestled and had a dip. When we came back we bought 28 eggs for seven packs of Old Golds. We boiled 'em and had a little feast. Matheson had a tooth pulled and so he's a little sick.

March 31, 1943

Laid down this afternoon because I had a headache that has been troubling me the last few days. Had the chills pretty bad last night.

Bill and Betty on Cairo souvenir.

Jarboe and Fay, sitting around doing nothing.

Home sweet home.

4. APRIL 1943

THE OIL FIELDS
OF PLOESTI

In England, Winston Churchill called Ploesti "the taproot of German might." The British War Cabinet had Ploesti high on their strike list. In Germany, Albert Speer warned Hitler that attacks on Germany's oil could halt the Reich's war production. In the United States, political and military strategists knew that this major source of Nazi oil would have to be taken out if Germany's war machine were to be halted. The refineries were well known by friend and foe alike.

The first refinery in Ploesti was opened in 1856. By 1943, this vital city with a population of 76,000 and situated about 35 miles north of Bucharest was encircled by approximately 40 refineries. These installations included eight of the world's largest and up-to-date refineries that produced over 400,000 tons of refined gasoline each year, or approximately one-third of Germany's supply of liquid fuel. The largest nine refineries were named: Astra Romana, Romana Americana (American-owned), Concordia Vega, Steaua Romana, Columbia Aquila, Dacia Romana, Creditul Minier, Standard & Unirea, and Xenia. Each refinery was quite large and covered several acres. Ploesti was one of three bottlenecks on the main railroad leading from the west to the Russian front, which made it a number one target.

The Ploesti raid of August 1, 1943 was not the first during World War II, nor was it going to be the last. German army units had come to Ploesti as early as the fall of 1940. In a short time Germany had taken over the refineries and appropriated the oil.

On June 23, 1941, the Russians bombed this critical area, and they tried again several times between 1941 and 1942, but inflicted little damage. On June 12, 1942, thirteen American B-24Ds took off from Fayid, Egypt, headed for Ploesti. Twelve made it to the target, but the bombs were dropped without clear sighting of the target due to clouds. Damage was minimal. Ironically, this raid alerted the Germans to the fact that Allied Forces were getting serious about going after the oil fields. Hitler, who had previously ignored the pleas of his generals, finally agreed to beef up the defenses at Ploesti.

By July 1943, more than 240 88mm guns were in place around the city. Hundreds of smaller caliber weapons were mounted on bridges, in towers, and under haystacks. Both north and south of the city, specially built flak trains sat on their tracks, ready to roll at a moment's notice. Just outside the city were installations of the latest-available radar equipment.

German fighter pilots were also on constant alert, as over 100 fighters (ME-109s, FW-190s and ME-110s) were spread over six airfields near Ploesti and three airfields near Bucharest. In addition, three squadrons of Romanian IAR80 and IAR81 fighters stood at the ready. By the time the 1943 raid was put into action, Ploesti was one of the most heavily defended German targets on the continent.

Since it was estimated that 60% of Germany's crude oil resources, or one-third of its supply of liquid fuel came from the Ploesti oil fields, knocking them out to some significant extent was critical to the war effort. On the eastern front, the Russian army was falling back against the Nazi onslaught. The Russians were only about 200 miles from Ploesti, and the German army needed Romanian oil to maintain their fighting apparatus against them. Among the Allied powers, it was believed that a good hit on Ploesti could shorten the war in Europe by as much as six months.

Once the German army was retreating out of North Africa, the Allied commanders decided to go after Ploesti. The oil-rich Romanian city, surrounded by refineries, corn fields and wheat fields, was a bomb attack waiting to happen.

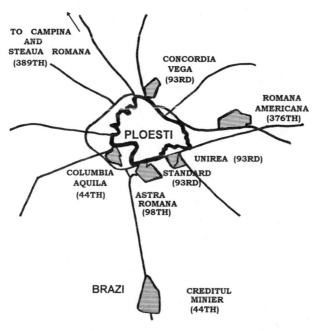

Figure 1. Layout of the Ploesti oil fields and targets assigned to the five bomb groups.

Two of Ploesti's refineries: Astra Romana (target of the 98th Bomb Group), and Standard (target of the 93rd). No. 1 is a stabilization plant; No. 2 is a distillation plant; No. 3 is a boiler house; and No. 4 is a pumping station. (National Archives Still Pictures)

FAY DIARY: April 1, 1943

Went over to Brown's tent and read the Minneapolis papers of Sunday the 3rd and the 10th. There was a huge fire a few miles away from camp. They believe it was a *Wimpy* that crashed.

April 2, 1943

We had news of a briefing. The target was Naples. We took off at 2:48. The weather was rugged and when we got there it was completely overcast. We flew over for more than an hour and there was a little break but the Colonel [Kane] didn't bomb. We had three pursuits on us at the time. Then en route home our bomb bay tank went dry before we knew it so we dropped our bombs in the water. We went off our course for about two hours.

We landed at L.G. 140 next to L.G. 159. It was an English field and they treated us swell with eggs, bread and jelly. We put in 700 gallons of gas and took off for home.

April 3, 1943

Landed at 1:00 this afternoon. Most of the squadron has already moved back to Benina. Rumors of a mission tomorrow.

April 4, 1943

We were told to pack and move back to Benina Main. I reckon we'll stay here for a couple of weeks and then pull anchor again.

Time to relax.

Not like Mom used to make.

Love that Spam!

A big smile for the folks back home.

April 5, 1943

Bought six eggs for two packages of Old Golds. Ate dinner and found out we had a briefing at noon. The target was the docks at Palermo. We took off at 2:15 pm but gas was leaking from numbers 2 and 3 engines pretty bad, so we had to turn back.

April 6, 1943

Charlie and I went into Benghazi and visited a church which was really beautiful. We came back and ate and everyone received mail but me and Jarboe.

April 7, 1943

Today's target was Palermo. We flew through a large cluster of clouds and it was really rough. We flew at 23,000 feet and bombed at 21,000. The ack-ack was really rugged. One ship had to land at Malta. We flew partly over a storm coming back. Our plane was **Old Baldy**, a new ship with the "demand system" in it. The temperature up there was 38 degrees below zero.

April 8, 1943

Found out that **Snafu** crashed. No one was killed except the pilot, who was killed over the target.

EXCERPT FROM DAVID GANDIN'S DIARY:

"Bill [Moffett] woke us at 0420—there had been a crash and **Snafu** was on fire. Marsh had been killed instantly by ack-ack while going over the target. His skull was crushed in. The top of the cockpit was also torn off. Blevins called down to Novack that Marsh was dead. Vengler came up with a walk-around bottle and removed Marsh from the pilot's seat. Blevins couldn't stand it with Marsh in the seat and all the blood flowing around.

"Blevins moved over to the pilot's seat and kept in the formation until they had to head off. All the compasses were out, so Novack had Blevins fly the opposite direction of the setting sun—all the men were freezing because of the hole in the top of the cockpit. The engineer was sick to his stomach from all the blood. The radio operator received QDMs both from Venina and Malta which were 211—obviously Nazi stations. Novack then flew just the opposite of the North Star and apparently passed over Crete where they received searchlights and ack-ack. Blevins' eyeball was scratched and Marsh's blood was frozen on his hands.

"At last they reached the Derma Beacon and proceeded to come into Benina. Blevins was on his first mission as was almost the remainder of the crew—and had never made a night landing before. As he came in, he banked too far to the left and knocked off the left landing gear, bounced over and did the same to the right one; the ship crash-landed and caught on fire. Thank God all got out OK, though Novack wouldn't leave till they took Marsh's body out also. The plane burned to a crisp."

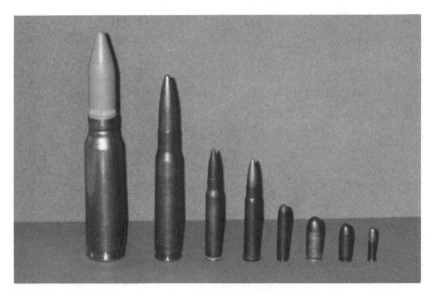

Shells used in World War II and up to present day. Left-to-right:

- 20 mm shell (6 ½ in. high) used by German fighters during the war. These were the shells that brought down **Maternity Ward** and many other American planes.
- 50 cal Browning shell (5 ½ in. high) used by U.S. B-24s.
- 30.06 cal U.S. rifle shell.
- 303 British rifle shell.
- 762x54R Russian rifle shell.
- 30 cal M-1 carbine U.S. shell.
- 45 cal acp U.S. pistol shell.
- 22 cal U.S. rifle shell.

FAY DIARY: April 9, 1943

Boiled myself about 15 eggs and then brought my bed inside after airing it out all morning. Bought a few cans of beans and two bottles of beer.

April 10, 1943

Woke up and they had French toast. It was the best breakfast I've had overseas.

April 11, 1943

Went to Naples. Take-off was 3:00 in the afternoon and we returned about 1:20 am. Ack-ack was rugged and we had about 12 pursuits after us. Three of them were believed destroyed. We lost one, which crashed in the sea. Three landed at Malta, one of which crash-landed. We got hit twice in the wing, and Matheson's top turret was completely demolished. Lucky he didn't get killed.

The Colonel [Kane] gave me a cigar for my birthday. When I came back I had three letters. One was from Betty. She informed me of her engagement. This is one birthday I won't forget.

April 12, 1943

Target today was Catania. We flew at 26,000 feet and all our oxygen masks froze up.

April 15, 1943

Received another letter from Betty informing me of "the news."

April 16, 1943

Missed chow and roll call. More than likely I'll catch hell tomorrow. After chow we fixed the backstop on our ball diamond. Had a game against the officers and beat them.

April 17, 1943

Had eight fried eggs and Spam.

April 27, 1943

Went for a swim at Berka 2 and ran into a Limey truck on the way back. Listened to the news and a lot of music.

April 28, 1943

Target was Messina. We carried 2,000-lb bombs. One ship got hit and went down in the Med, but all were saved and are in a hospital in Malta. A few others got hit and had a sweating-out time coming back.

April 29, 1943

Went to the club and listened to some records on a portable Victrola.

April 30, 1943

Gandy and I went swimming and came back about 4:30. We have a mission for tomorrow. Harris asked me to instruct the new crew on oxygen and things in general.

5. MAY 1943

PLANNING THE RAID

By 1942, the importance of slowing down the German war machine was uppermost in the minds of U.S. Army Air Forces' high command. In January 1943 Winston Churchill and Franklin Roosevelt met in Casablanca to put together a new war strategy, which included moving into Sicily and Italy. The resulting "Casablanca Directive" outlined future American and British Bomber Command operations, and one of the targets high on the list of the Combined Chiefs of Staff was oil installations.

Serious planning to go after Ploesti began in March 1943. Those in charge were General H. H. Arnold, Chief of the Air Corps, Lt. Col. Whitney of the 9th Air Force, and Col. Jacob E. Smart of General Arnold's advisory council. Certain facts were known: considering the size of the refinery area, effective high-altitude bombing would require at least 1,000 long-range bombers. This large number made it impossible. Low-altitude bombing was a different story. It was thought that fewer planes could do the job if experienced pilots and crews were available to come to North Africa. In June 1943, General Dwight D.

Eisenhower, Commander-in-Chief of the North African Theater, approved a low-altitude bombing mission. Because of the large area covered by the refineries and the limited number of planes and bombs, the planners chose certain structures to be specific targets: boiler houses, distilling units and cracking towers. Properly identified, it would be possible to spot them visually and bomb them at a low altitude.

According to intelligence reports from various sources, German ground defenses were located mainly south of the refineries. The plan was therefore to send B-24s across Romania to a point northwest of the target, have them turn back, drop their bombs, and return to Benghazi. It was approximately 1,200 miles from base to target, or roughly 2,500 miles round-trip.

Could the B-24 do the job? Col. Jacob Smart and Lt. Col. W. Lesley Forster believed they could. These planes were big and rugged, long-range, and had proved themselves many times. They would also have the advantage of coming in under radar coverage. If the element of surprise could be achieved, few enemy fighters would be in the air and those that were would have difficulty attacking anything so low. The big German artillery on the ground was designed to go after high-altitude flying, and would have difficulty tracking fast-moving planes coming toward them at tree-top level. Gunners on the B-24s could shoot back. Planes that were in trouble could attempt to crash-land on nearly flat ground (no one could bail out at such a low altitude). Col. Smart decided the plan was feasible, and so a never-before-tried, low-level bombing attack was given the go-ahead.

Major General Lewis H. Brereton, commander of the 9th Air Force and the man in charge of conducting the operation, said that even if not one plane returned, the mission would be considered a success. He saw this attack as the "final knockout blow" against Germany. All crews were told they were expendable. Losses were expected to be 50%. Seven of the nine major refineries were chosen as targets. Of the five participating bomb groups, three were given one target each and two were given two targets each. The name chosen for this mission was *"Operation Tidal Wave."*

FAY DIARY: May 1, 1943

I had a shot. My arm doesn't feel very good.

Target today was Reggio Calabria, and it was a complete overcast. We had about 65 planes and the clouds were so bad we couldn't see the plane next to us. It was really a miracle that no one collided.

May 2, 1943

Gandy woke me and told me Harris didn't get back last night. It is believed that another plane crashed into him up in the clouds. It's really hard to take because we were really close friends. He and the co-pilot who was new were due to be papas. We talked it over and as there's nothing anyone can do we'll have to forget it, but I'll always remember him.

May 3, 1943

They held a session concerning the two missing planes. It is believed that only one crashed into the sea and the other one, which probably was Harris, may have landed in enemy territory. I'm hoping to hear about Harris and pray that he's safe.

May 4, 1943

Egan came over and told us to be on the alert. Take-off was at 11:30, and the target was Reggio. Because of clouds we couldn't find it and had to come down as our oxygen supply was almost exhausted. We came back through a storm and it's a wonder we didn't lose any ships.

May 5, 1943

A telegram came saying that Harris' wife had an 8-lb baby boy. His things are being sent home.

May 6, 1943

Target was Reggio Harbor. Ack-ack was pretty accurate; one ship from the 343rd was lost. Some pretty good hits were seen on the target, and I threw out two boxes of incendiaries.

Tore off Gleason's oxygen mask and saw what happened just in time to save him. Egan passed out over the target and Stallings flew the plane. Wes has sand fly fever and so that means we'll lose some time this week.

May 7, 1943

A new order is that we have to carry our rifles and helmets everywhere and at all times.

May 8, 1943

Stood roll call and then Gandy and I went to the hospital to see Egan. He was still nursing a fever. Heard that Bizerta and Tunis fell. Looks like a mission tomorrow, but I don't believe we'll go as Egan won't be back for a few days.

May 9, 1943

Paid Egan a visit then went to Benghazi. They had mass and benediction for Mother's Day.

May 10, 1943

There was a briefing and the target was Naples, but we were not slated to go as "The Beaver" isn't back from the hospital yet.

View from Bill Fay's waist-gunner's window.

Highlight of the day (Fay, Matheson and Chiverton).

Always standing in line.

May 11, 1943

The boys took off for a mission, but the target was changed to Catania. One of the 415th 's planes had to land at Malta as someone got hit. Charlie and I paid "The Beaver" a visit, then we went into Benghazi and ate. Came back and saw the picture "King's Row."

May 12, 1943

Heard some talk about us bombing Greece. After supper we went to the Beaver's tent and was informed that our crew and the mess officers were going to Cairo and Tel Aviv to get supplies. They lost **Zombie** from the 415th.

May 13, 1943

Went out to the plane and as we were ready to take off the tower called and told us to go back. They had to have that ship for a mission. We waited until noon as they were patching some ack-ack and bullet holes on **Cindy**. We took off and it was a rather rough ride. We let Jack and Jr. off at Cairo and proceeded to Tel Aviv. We landed there about 6:00 pm and went into town. Got a room at the Red Cross and after a shower we went hunting. Charlie and I picked up a couple of Pole German refugees and had a good time. We then went back and picked up a couple of French lasses and then went home about 3:00 am. Pop had too much to drink and could hardly walk.

May 14, 1943

All combat crews were taken out and had photos taken of their plane and crews. We ate and then Beaver told us to come over to his tent tonight to celebrate his First Lieutenant.

May 15, 1943

Went to the Beaver's tent after supper and celebrated Moffett's and Beaver's First Lieutenant. We had three bottles of champagne and about three bottles of beer. We all got feeling pretty high and really slung the shit.

Went to mass about 4:00 pm. Captain Eddie Rickenbacker stopped off here and gave us a pep talk.

May 18, 1943

Heard we may be getting decorated tomorrow morning. Went to watch a ball game then came back and copied a few poems I believe to be interesting.

May 20, 1943

Got up and started to get dressed as the General was due here to give out awards. Then they told us there was a mission so we changed back to our flying clothes. We changed back and forth and finally both occasions were canceled.

May 21, 1943

Took off on a mission and the target was Reggio. There was a partial front and we lost our formation. We joined up with two ships from Lete and three of us went over the target. The ack-ack was pretty well aimed. Eight planes went over ahead of us and were pretty well shot up by enemy aircraft. Two boys in the 415th were wounded.

May 23, 1943

Went into Benghazi and looked around. They opened up the theater at 8:00 pm. Talked to some *Kiwis* coming back from Tunis and they certainly don't love the British.

A Raving

Once upon a mission dreary
  When of combat I'd grown weary,
I had flown a thousand hours
  And was sure to fly some more.

Suddenly there came a knocking
  Sounded like some ack-ack popping,
Popping like the very devil
  Just beneath my bomb bay door.

"T'is some Jerry," thought I,
  "Who's wishing to improve his score.
I will use evasive tactics
  Even if he does get sore."

Turning then, I saw before me
  Blacker now then e'er before,
Ack-ack bursting close and heavy
  Guess I'd better turn some more.

Opening wide I swung the bomb bay doors,
  And to my surprise and horror,
Flashing fast and bright below me
  Were some ninety guns or more.

And above the shrapnel's screeching,
  I remembered then the briefing--
When they told me with much speaking
  There was only three or four!

Leveling then I made a bomb run
  Which was not a very long one,
For the Varsity was on duty
  And I'd seen their work before.

Then our engine coughed and clattered,
  And the glass around me splattered
And I knew they had my number,
  Just my number, nothing more.

Then at last the bombs were toggled
  And alone away I hobbled,
With some fifty-seven inches
  And a feathered number four.

While outside like ducks migrating
  Was a drove of M.E.s waiting,
Waiting all with itching fingers
  Set to even up the score.

I had lost my upper turret,
  And alone, defenseless worried.
I was the saddest creature
  Mortal woman ever bore.

For each bright and screaming tracer,
  Coming nearer, ever nearer
Made my spirits sink within me,
  Just my spirits, nothing more.

Then at last to my elation
  I caught up with my formation
And the M.E.s turned and left me
  By the tens and by the score.

But my wings were torn and tattered,
  And my nerves completely shattered.
And as far as I'm concerned
  The war is o'er.

Now my sinus starts to seeping,
  Every time they mention briefing.
And for this they'll change my brass
  to double bars.

And I have my fun and frolic
  And a case of combat colic,
Here in Cairo with the Cossacks,
  Among the Eagles and the Stars.

Now I've learned the act of living,
  And my secret I am giving
To the rest of those among you
  Who might care to live some more.

For my sinus still is seeping,
  Every time they mention briefing.
No more flying, no more missions,
  No more combat, never more.

            2/Lt. William S. Robinson
            Gambut, 2-27-43 *

*A carbon copy of this poem was found
 in the private papers of Bill Fay.

Some serious talk by (L-R) Chiverton, Jarboe, Matheson, Fay, and German (man with glasses unknown).

Getting ready to pilot the big bird.

May 24, 1943

Went to a briefing. The target was San Giovanni. We took off at 9:40 am. Halpro hit Reggio a few minutes before we reach San Giovanni, and we saw huge fires. Our hits were really good and we practically demolished the place. We landed at 5:40 pm and everything was OK.

May 25, 1943

We were briefed for Messina. We took off at 10 bells and hit the target about 2:36 pm. The ack-ack was really rough and we received about 40 holes. Mike (German) got hit in the side and Pop [Chiverton] and I just missed getting hit when we bent over to throw out the cindies and a piece came through the plane.

Our bomb bay was hit and gas flew all over the place. Pop [Chiverton] fixed it at 20,000 feet and saved the day. It was lucky it didn't explode and I guess we prayed enough. We had to land at Malta where we were interrogated and Mike was taken to the hospital. Dore's crew also landed there and three other planes from the 98th. One fellow was killed and one had a punctured lung. One also had his head blown off.

EXCERPT FROM DAVID GANDIN'S DIARY, May 25, 1943:

We were at 20,000 and dropping when the "old man" took off his own chute and oxygen mask, went into the bomb bay, which was filled with gas fumes, and switched tanks. He called Wes to switch off the booster pump and feather No. 2. The rest of the engines started doing O.K. When Pop came back Sgt. Fay slapped his face to knock the grogginess out of him. Jarboe had gotten out of the turret because gas had streamed all over it. Then Pop saw where the leak was coming from; the bomb bay hose was cut badly. He took the compress and tourniquet from a first-aid kit and tied it around the leak. It worked.

Meanwhile, Stallings climbed out of the co-pilot's seat to give first aid to Mike [German], who was wounded in the left side by a piece of ack-ack. Wes called and said to go to Malta. I took him far enough south of Sicily to not be intercepted by enemy fighters. The ship was in bad shape, and we wanted to get Mike to a hospital as quickly as possible.

FAY DIARY: May 26, 1943

Went out to the plane and looked it over. The wing was cracked and full of holes. Went into town and saw Mike. They took the shrapnel out but they were feeding him through the I.V. for shock and possible internal injuries. He may be there for six or eight weeks. They sent in a request for a Silver Star for Pop.

May 27, 1943

Went to a movie at camp entitled, "A Tale of Two Cities," but it started to rain and the wind blew down the screen so we didn't see the whole show.

May 28, 1943

Took off at 8:10. The weather wasn't too good and the No. 3 engine cut out on us a few times. Today we went over the 200-hour mark.

May 30, 1943

Took off at 9:00. We hit the target [Foggia, Italy] at 2:00 and along the way we dumped four boxes of cindies. The hits looked pretty good on the target. The ack-ack was heavy, but it was our level.

It's a lonely life.

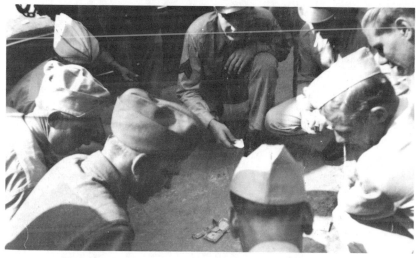

Evening's entertainment. Man at top, center, is Lt. Andrew L. Anderson, co-pilot of **Maternity Ward**.

The 98th's **Boiler Maker II** on a run.

Boiler Maker II, Ser.No. 41-23782-E, was piloted by Theodore Helin on the Ploesti mission. The plane crashed in a cornfield in Romania, and all crew members were held as P.O.W.s in Romania until the war's end.

Boiler Maker II nose art.

Lil Joe, Ser. No. 41-11886-S, was piloted by Lindley Hussey on the Ploesti mission. the plane crashed in Romania where five crew members were killed and the pilot and three others held as prisoners-of-war.

Chug-A-Lug, Ser. No. 41-11766-V, was piloted by LeRoy Morgan during the Plosti mission. While in flight two crew members were wounded and one, James Van Ness, was killed.

Pluto, of the 345th Sqdn, Ser. No. 41-23715W, crashed in bad weather over Italy and was never heard from again. The pilot, Marion Harris, formerly was co-pilot with the crew of **Lil Joe**. Several B-24s were named after Disney characters.

B-24 nose art.

Pink Lady, Ser. No. 41-11798-F, piloted by Captain McHugh, was lost on a mission over Naples on March 18, 1943

Floogie Boo, sometimes called **Floogie Boo Bird**, Ser. No. 41-11810-C, was a troublesome plane that was eventually overhauled and given a new name.

Daisy Mae, Ser. No. 41-11815, was piloted by Lewis N. Ellis of the 389th on the Ploesti mission and flew with a crew from the 389th. The plane returned safely but two crew members were wounded.

B-24 nose art.

80

Zombie, Ser. No. 41-11787-D of the 415th Sqdn, was lost on May 11, 1943, on a mission to Catania with Captain Ingerson piloting the ship.

Old Baldy of the 345th Ser. No. 42-40102-T, was piloted by John Dore, Jr., during the Ploesti mission. Unfortunately the plane went down and all crew members were killed.

Snafu, Ser. No. 41-24275-U, of the 345th was piloted by Captain Marsh on an April 7, 1943 mission to Palermo. Marsh was struck in the head by German cannon fire and killed instantly. **Snafu** returned to Benina Main where it crash-landed with co-pilot Hilary Blevins bringing it in at night. All remaining crew members escaped safely. (See diary entry of April 7.)

B-24 nose art.

Fertile Myrtle, of the 415th, Ser. No.41-24023-J, was piloted by Herbert Shingler, Jr., during the Ploesti mission. The plane returned safely.

Chief, (early art) Ser. No. 41-11774-0, piloted by Thomas Fravega of the 345th on the Ploesti mission with a crew from the 389th, also returned safely.

Li'l De-Icer, Ser. No. 41-11836-I, one of Bill Fay's earlier planes, flew with pilot James Merrick on the Ploesti mission and returned safe

B-24 nose art.

6. JUNE 1943

GETTING READY

Col. Smart of General Arnold's advisory council met with British Prime Minister Winston Churchill, who approved the plan for the low-level raid. He then recruited Col. Ted Timberlake's experienced 93rd Bomb Group, called the "Flying Circus," that would be led by Col. Addison Baker. They would be joining Col. Keith Compton's 376th Bomb Group, the "Liberandos"; Col. John R. Kane's 98th Bomb Group, the "Pyramidiers"; Col. Leon Johnson's 44th Bomb Group, the "Flying Eight Balls"; and Col. Jack Wood's 389th Bomb Group, the "Sky Scorpions." Maps of the surrounding countryside were obtained and marked with certain "*I.P.*s," or initial points, to be used by navigators to find their way to the target. Navigating at low altitudes was very difficult, as everything in sight rushed by so fast. Trees and valleys looked like a blur, so it would be easy to make a wrong turn. To help the crews when the planes reached the target, drawings of specific buildings were made so that each refinery layout could be targeted specifically and the bombing would be accurate. An intricate scale model of Ploesti was built to familiarize the men who would be flying over this complicated landscape.

Bombing assignments were divided up as follows: The 376th Bomb Group, the oldest and most experienced in the Mediterranean area, was given "Target White I," or the Romana Americana refinery. Theirs would be the lead formation. Following the 376th would be the 93rd, which had "Targets White II and III" as their objective (Concordia Vega, Standard Petrol Block, and Unirea Speranta refineries). The 98th would be headed for "Target White IV" and the largest of the refineries (Astra Romana), and the 44th received two targets: "White V" (Columbia Aquila) and "Blue" (Creditul Minier). Creditul Minier was located away from the central Ploesti refineries at a place called Brazi. Last but not least, the 389th, the newest group, would go after "Target Red," another separate compound located at Campina. (See flight plan diagram on page 53.) Each plane was given a single target to bomb within its assigned refinery.

The five bomb groups converged on the North African desert during the first few months of 1943. Flight crews set up shop in this largely empty land, wondering what was in store for them. Although the men in charge of planning the mission knew what was going to happen, the officers and enlisted men could only speculate about the size and location of the operation. It was clear they were close to German-occupied Italy and Greece, but Ploesti was only a rumor and seemed a remote if not impossible target.

Assorted raids were scheduled for Messina, Sicily, Naples, and other occupied areas. On July 9 the 389th flew a mission to Malame, Crete, where one of their planes was lost to German fighters. Flight crews attended briefings for short-range attacks, but few knew about the big plan.

On July 20, the five group commanders met in secrecy. All were not enthusiastic about the low-altitude plan, including Generals Brereton and Ent, who would have preferred high-altitude attacks. Each commander was told the overall strategy and instructed to devise the actual battle plan for his group.

Crews began test runs to determine how far a fully loaded B-24 could fly. Test bombs were dropped at low altitudes to see how accurate they would be. These large planes flew so low that they scattered sheep and knocked over tents. They took turns flying very close to the ground, first alone and then in formation. The pilots had to learn to keep control of the planes that were affected by severe prop wash and vibration that occurred at such low altitudes and in such tight formation. Wing-tip vortices wreaked havoc with planes in such close proximity to each other. Swirling sand kicked up by the prop wash blew directly into the engines, causing serious mechanical problems.

All the planes were tested and modified. Three additional 50-caliber machine guns, to be controlled by the pilot, were installed in the nose above the bombsight for this mission. Norden bombsights were replaced by a modified version of a gunsight specially calibrated for low-level bombing. New temporary 400-gallon gas tanks were installed in bomb bays. Older planes were patched extensively. The older planes were generally painted desert sand pink, while the newer ones were various shades of green.

On July 24, most officers were told about the planned Ploesti mission. Rumors had been flying for days that the oil fields would be the logical target, although some of the pilots still thought it might be the hydroelectric dams in Germany. On July 28, General Ent issued the following battle order: "The 9th U.S. Air Force will attack and destroy the seven principal oil refineries in the Ploesti area on 1 August 1943, employing seven target forces in a minimum altitude attack in order to deny the enemy use of the petroleum products processed in that area." Ploesti would be the only bombing raid conducted during World War II that would be classified as a campaign in itself.

FAY DIARY: June 1, 1943

Went out to the plane and Deacon, myself, Moon, Yeiser, Weber, and a new Lt. Sternfels went for a test hop. After supper Charlie and I went into Benghazi to see "Rio Rita."

June 3, 1943

Charlie and I started for Benghazi about 10:30. We ran into some fellows from the 376th and went to the theater and saw "Sailors Three," a Limey film.

June 6, 1943

Drank some wine to celebrate Gandy's and Pete's First Lieutenant.

June 8, 1943

Lt. Bogart came to our tent about 1:00 am and told Pop and me to get ready for decoration tomorrow. We woke up about 7:00 and after borrowing enough clothes that were clean we went to the tower. We got there at 8:30 and waited until about 11:00 for General Brereton. Fourteen of us were decorated, including Col. Killer Kane and Major Jones.

June 13, 1943

Had a mission and the target was Catania. The ack-ack was heavy and we had fighter escort from Malta. Stone and K.K. [Phillips] collided in mid-air about two hours from base. They crashed in the sea and no one was saved. Major Jones, Captain Stone, Captain Ahlo, Captain Lemars, and Moffett our bombardier were down. We circled and I saw one man in the sea. We then went to Malta and Egan and Gandy and Math went out in a flying boat, but could not locate any survivors.

EXCERPT FROM DAVID GANDIN'S DIARY, June 13, 1943:

"We took off here at 0935 and were supposed to meet a top cover of Spitfires at 1300 hours over the target. We ran into bad weather and steered west of the front and then turned north. Charles went up to over 22,000 feet but we still managed to just keep on top of it. K.K. did a nice job of taking us through it. When it finally cleared below we saw Sicily to the left. We reached our initial point at about 1300 and started toward the Catania Airdrome. Six Spits crossed our nose and one of our inexperienced gunners fired at them.

"As we closed into the target area we saw the other airdrome in smoke and flames, just bombed by the 376th Bomb Group. Phillips' element went over the target first and we crossed over next to the left. Ack-ack was heavy and all around but we weren't hit even once. We dropped our bombs at 1314, waited a good ten seconds for our wing men to drop, and then made a slow turn to the left—over the opposite airdrome. Our bombs missed the pinpoint but still did considerable damage. Ack-ack didn't bother us too much after that. We were attacked by pursuit, ME's and 190's, but only one broke through the top cover and did no damage.

"The real danger finally over, we settled down the easy job of going home. We were leading the 2nd element. Suddenly, at 1435, I felt Wes [Egan] swing left.

"I couldn't believe what I saw: two B-24's in flat spins diving straight for the sea—and a rudder flying here, an elevator there. It was over in a few short seconds—10 seconds at the most. I saw them crash into the sea and disappear. Some wreckage came to the surface; many oxygen bottles floated to the surface, and there was an oil slick.

"We buzzed and circled. Fay said he spotted one man circling. I figured a DR position of 35 degrees 20'N; 18 degrees 10'E, at 1444 hours, and we headed straight to Malta.

"We radioed Malta to have Air Sea Rescue ships ready. Landed at Malta at 1600 and boarded a Sunderland flying boat. We hit the oil slick on the head at 1918 and searched and searched, to no avail. All we could see were a couple of oxygen bottles and a few scraps of wreckage. All along, Wes and I thought it was Stone and Sternfels—and Bill [Moffett] was with K.K. [Phillips]. After a good search—thoroughly convinced of no remaining lives, we went back to Malta and to bed, where nightmare after nightmare gave me problems all night."

SURVIVING A TOUR OF DUTY

The significance of counting down hours for completing a tour of duty is portrayed in the graph on the following page. It shows the probability of an airman surviving after flying a fixed number of missions ("N"), assuming that: 1) a fixed number of planes per mission (attrition rate of 2%, 5%, 10% and 33% for illustration) are destroyed with no survivors; 2) no airmen are killed if the plane survives; and the chance of any given plane being destroyed is the same.

Since a tour of duty is based on hours, certain simple assumptions have been made to convert flight hours to one flight mission. Based on the approximate B-24 range of 2500 miles and a typical plane-to-ground speed of 250 mph, 10 hours of flight time translates to one mission. Thus, an airman has to survive 30 missions to complete a tour of duty equivalent to 300 hours.

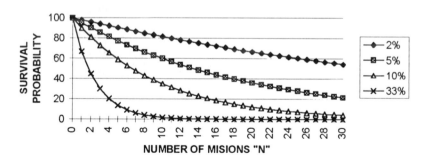

PROBABILITY OF SURVIVING "N" MISSIONS WITH
VARIOUS SINGLE MISSION CASUALTY RATES

Figure 2. Probability of Survival

In the graph, starting from the top, the curves refer to the probability of surviving "N" missions, if every mission casualty rate is 2%, 5%, 10% and 33%, respectively.

Casualty Rate	Airmen Who Would Survive a Tour of 30 Missions
2%	55%
5%	21%
10%	4%
33%	0%

Thus, if there were ever to be casualty rates as high as 33% there would be no survivors, effectively resulting in the tour being a "suicide tour."

During World War II, acceptable American and English casualty rates were 5% (one out of 20 planes not returning), meaning that four out of five airmen would not survive a tour of 30 missions.

The German military's position on an air raid was that it was not possible to stop an aircraft from dropping its bombs on a target. Their goal was to cause the casualty rate to be high enough so that the Allies would reconsider their bombing strategy. This approach was somewhat successful with the English, in that they eventually stopped daytime bombing and accepted lower accuracy with nighttime raids. The Americans continued daylight raids.

FAY DIARY: June 14, 1943

Woke up about 8:00 and went out to the plane. We saw three Spits crack up. We took off about 1:00 and landed at our base about 3:30. Everyone is on guard because they [Germans] dropped 50 to 100 paratroopers somewhere over here. I told them about the sub I saw and the little boat. I just can't believe that Moffett's gone.

EXCERPT FROM DAVID GANDIN'S DIARY, June 15, 1943:

"Wes and I packed up Bill's things to be sent home. Everything I see and touch is a remembrance of Bill; his laugh and smile, how the two of us were going to "snow 'em under" when we returned to the States. Bill, his good heart and ever-helping hand. I can't help but cry. It's going to be so terribly hard to write to his family.

"The damage at Catania Airdrome was severe. The element Bill led hit the pinpoint targets of hangars and dispersed aircraft. Bill's last job—a blaze of glory."

FAY DIARY: June 17, 1943

Woke up and ate then had a briefing. The target was Biscari Airdrome [Sicily]. We took off at 10:00 and a few ships turned back and we had to fill in another slot. We had about 50 Spit escorts. The ack-ack was heavy, but over to one side. We almost bombed another formation who turned below us. Hit the target at 1:33.

June 18, 1943

Woke up and found out that one Wimpy, three P-40s, and one B-24 [**Arkansas Traveler**] were blown up by those German paratroopers. [There has always been speculation that **Arkansas Traveler** was inadvertently destroyed by fire that resulted from American troops cleaning the plane with gasoline that caught on fire.] Found a note left by the Beaver that there is a briefing tomorrow morning. He's been made Operations Officer.

June 19, 1943

Briefing was held at 8:15. We took off at 10:35 for Reggio. The clouds were numerous and the formations got all mixed up. There was a lot of ack-ack and about four or five fighters. I believe I hit one a few times.

June 20, 1943

Two guards were killed at Lete. One was clubbed to death, the other stabbed by the German paratroopers. We had a briefing and the target was San Giovanni.

June 21, 1943

Took off at 9:25. We were attacked by about 20 pursuits and had our front tire shot up. Our left wing man was hit and we landed at Malta. When we came back Egan made a very good landing. Our ground crew was worried. I hit one ME. We were credited with two enemy aircraft and one probable.

June 22, 1943

Charlie and I went to gunnery school. Went and saw the "Yacht Club Boys" (band) and they weren't any too hot as they were pretty plastered.

June 24, 1943

Had a briefing at 5:00. The target was the airdrome at Salonika [Greece]. No ack-ack or pursuits were encountered. There were a lot of good hits and we took them by surprise.

June 25, 1943

Looked at the pictures of our raid yesterday and it was very good. One of the 343rd's ships blew up as we were on our way to the target.

June 27, 1943

Briefing at 7:00 and the target was Athens. We took off about 9:30. There was ack-ack and four pursuits. A few of our ships were damaged, they just missed us. Had chow and went to the movie and saw "I Got 'Em Covered." The generator burned out after half the reel was run and so we just saw half.

June 28, 1943

Helped unload rations. I helped on K.P. to feed about 300 men who just arrived from England.

June 29, 1943

Saw "You Can't Fool Your Wife." The sound was terrible.

Letting loose over the target.
(Smithsonian Institution)

7. JULY 1943

FINAL PREPARATION
AND ANTICIPATION

July 30, 1943. The big event was only two days away. All crew members had now been briefed and warned: 50% were not expected to return. That meant either you or your buddy would die or be wounded and shot down somewhere between base and target--not an easy thing to think about. Letters to family members and loved ones were written and set aside to be mailed if the men didn't come back. Affairs were put in order as these now-seasoned combat crews met with chaplains and friends, maybe for the last time.

There was no lack of activity, however, as ground crews worked feverishly on the planes and flight crews took them up for final test runs. Crew rosters were put together, and no one was allowed to go home, even if they had put in their 300 hours flying time. Every ounce of energy was aimed at carrying out the biggest mission ever, and it was both frightening and exciting. Adrenaline was pumping and most men had no second thoughts about being assigned to the mission. There was one problem, however. Quite a few crew members came down with dysentery, and many flight crews were short-staffed. Substitutes were assigned where needed, some of whom had received only minimal briefing. Bill Fay was one of the substitutes.

As the big day drew near, a full-scale practice was held. The entire complement of B-24s in tight formation flew out over the Mediterranean and bombed a practice target. It was a sight to behold. The run went perfectly, giving confidence to those in the air and on the ground.

Finally, the men received encouragement from the commanding officers. General Brereton spoke to each of the five bomb groups' commanders and combat crews, saying that he was satisfied with the practice runs and telling them that they could accomplish in one day what would take ground forces at least one year. His statement to the 98th was: "We expect our losses to be 50%, but even though we should lose everything we've sent, but hit the target, it will be worth it." Eddie Rickenbacker stepped up to give the troops a pep talk, then Col. John "Killer" Kane spoke specifically to the flight crews of the 98th. He vowed to lead them to the target in one of the most important missions they would ever fly.

The men knew their lives were expendable and that there was a good chance their plane would go down over Romania. Every man was given a survival pack in case he ended up trying to make his way out on foot. Much was said about getting to and destroying the target, but little was said about making it back to base. Some were afraid but dare not let their feelings be known. Others were optimistic and planned for their return. Most laid out their flight suits before they hit the sack. Few could sleep, however, and many stayed up all night. The lucky ones managed to drift off for a few precious hours.

FAY DIARY: July 1, 1943

Mission to the Taranto airdrome was called off.

July 2, 1943

Ate chow and got ready to take off. Our No. 2 engine cut out and so we didn't get off. The raid was a success, but I believe five planes were lost from the 44th and 98th. I don't know if the 376th or 93rd lost any as yet. Went into town with Egan and took a shower. After chow we went and saw "They Got Me Covered." It stunk.

July 3, 1943

I gave Charlie a haircut--whoa! We went into Benghazi and had chow and hitchhiked to the swimming pool. Gandy, Pop and Math also came out.

July 5, 1943

Took off at 8:45 and the target was Messina. The ack-ack was heavy and only about eight pursuits. We received about 10 holes. Over 100 planes took part in the raid. Good hits were made on our target.

July 6, 1943

Went to the hospital with a touch of malaria.

July 7, 1943

The rest of my crew finished their 300 hours and I have 10 hours and 15 minutes left.

July 8-15, 1943

[Bill Fay was in the hospital with malaria.]

July 16, 1943

Got out of the hospital this afternoon, but I'm still grounded. Pop is here, but the rest went on a *jig-jig run.*

July 17, 1943

Went to see the doc and he said I was still grounded. They had a raid today, the target was Naples. One 44th ship went down.

July 18, 1943

Helped unload a truck of supplies. Still grounded.

July 23, 1943

We took off for Tripoli to pick up another crew. It's a nice place and we had cold drinks with real ice.

AUTHOR'S NOTE:

There were no more entries in Bill Fay's diary after July 23. Bill had a little over 10 hours flying time left to complete his 300 hours. Tension in the camp was building for the August 1 Ploesti raid. Still feeling the effects of his malaria, he nevertheless kept asking his commanding officer, Lt. Wes Egan, to be put on a B-24 headed to the oil fields. His wish was granted, and he was assigned to Lt. John Ward's ship, **Maternity Ward,** as a substitute gunner.

Clearing the smoke after a successful bombing raid.
(National Archives Still Pictures)

Desert footgear.

Checking the coordinates.

8. AUGUST 1943

TAKE-OFF

Dawn of the big day—August 1. It was a beautiful clear morning. At 0400 hours alarms sounded, voices were heard yelling calls and commands, and assorted vehicles began rumbling through the camps as crew members scrambled to climb into their flight gear and get ready to head out to the planes. Flight crews carried a heavy load of gear: flight suits, parachutes, navigation equipment, and whatever else they needed for their particular job.

Bill Fay was one of more than 1,700 men who trudged to the mess tents, ate breakfast in a subdued, almost reverent atmosphere, and prayed that he and his crew would return safely. The five B-24 bomb groups, consisting of 178 planes, were lined up awaiting their flight crews. The loud roar of warming engines penetrated the morning air as men began gathering around intelligence and operations huts for last-minute instructions.

A conveyance truck showed up, and Bill headed out to pick up his parachute and report to his assigned ship, **Maternity Ward**. The 10-man crew consisted of: Lt. John V. Ward, pilot; Lt. Andrew L. Anderson, co-pilot; Lt. Beverly S. Huntley, navigator; Lt. Henry C. Crump, Jr., bombardier; Tech Sgt. James J. Toth, top turret gunner; Staff Sgt. Kenneth L. Turner, gunner; Tech Sgt. Leon D. Pemberton, radio operator; Staff Sgt. Harold W. Scott, gunner, Staff Sgt. Robert E. Long, tail gunner; and Staff Sgt. William J. Fay, waist gunner. All but three were original members of **Maternity Ward**'s crew. Due to the illness of three of Ward's men, however, Pemberton, Scott and Fay had been assigned as last-minute substitutes.

Ground crews had spent all night working on the B-24s, making sure they were outfitted with everything they needed, including full fuel tanks (3,100 gallons of high octane). Each plane carried a full complement of demolition bombs plus boxes of British incendiaries that would be used to ignite refinery fires. The bombs consisted of both 1,000-lb and 500-lb units, and all were equipped with delay fuses. Bombs to be dropped by the first and second waves carried delays of 1-to-6 hours, and the last wave had bombs with only 45-second delay fuses. If the mission went as planned, all of the planes would be out of range before any of the bombs went off.

The big ships, standing like sentinels in the desert, sported shiny windshields that had been scrubbed and scrubbed again. Ground crews had thoroughly "pre-flighted" the planes, and the flight crews would do another pre-flight. Equipment had been cleaned and oiled, and sand had been brushed off ammo link belts to help keep them from jamming. Great care had been taken to replace aging engines and other parts that might cause problems. Holes had been patched. Each plane was in as good condition as possible for the big attack. As morning fast approached, there was little more the ground crews could do than stand back, often with tears in their eyes, hoping their ships and crews would make it home to Benghazi later that day in one piece.

Truck after truck pulled alongside the planes as flight crews arrived. With minimum conversation, these neatly attired men, who had carefully laid out their flight clothing only hours before, climbed aboard their Liberators and went through their pre-flight equipment check and inspection. Many of these young crew members were facing combat for the first time.

As the dawn began to break over the desert horizon to meet a clear blue sky, most of the men took a last walk across the sand greeting friends, shaking hands, and planning to meet when they returned that evening. They then walked around their planes, checking the exteriors for trouble spots. For many of them it would be the last walk they would take anywhere on earth. Finally, when everything appeared to be in order, they climbed back into the planes and settled into place. After all the preparation and practice, the big mission was about to begin.

Finally, engines roared to life and the heavily laden planes began to form up. By now the planes were hot and the interiors stifling. Air flowing through the flight decks was welcomed by the pilots. At 0700 the five bomb groups began taking off in the following order:

First: 376th Liberandos (28 planes) led by Col. Keith K. Compton and Brigadier General Uzal Ent

Second: 93rd Flying Circus (37 planes) led by Col. Addison Baker

Third: 98th Pyramidiers (48 planes) led by Col. John R. Kane

Fourth: 44th Flying 8-Balls (36 planes) led by Col. Leon W. Johnson

Fifth: 389th Sky Scorpions (29 planes) led by Col. Jack Wood.

General Brereton was supposed to fly with Col. Compton in the lead mission plane, but officials in Washington vetoed the idea and General Ent took his place. It was too risky sending the critically briefed Brereton on a mission where he could become a valuable prisoner of the Germans.

It was an awesome sight--178 magnificent ships, in various shades of pink and green, some new and ready for anything, others older and full of repairs, slowly ascending and circling the desert as they found their place in formation. At 0800 they headed out to sea, departing the Cyrenaica coast. It would be a long journey of more than seven hours over water and land, past the island of Corfu and over Albania and Yugoslavia, to the oil-rich city of Ploesti, Romania.

9. HELL IN THE AIR

It wasn't long before one of the planes was in serious trouble. Only a few minutes into the flight, **Kickapoo**, of the 98th Bomb Group, had an engine go out and tried to get back for an emergency landing. The bombs had been toggled before the plane started its descent, but as it approached the runway it hit high tension wires and a concrete telephone pole, broke apart and crashed. Only two crew members escaped the burning wreckage.

Undaunted by the tragedy of **Kickapoo,** which by now was burning on the edge of the Benina Main runway, the rest of the B-24s climbed into the sky and headed out over the Mediterranean. **Maternity Ward** was one of the 47 remaining planes of the 98th Pyramidiers. Second Lt. John Ward's plane flew in the fourth line (wave) of five, as Major Delbert Hahn's left wing man. Major Hahn, flying **Blackjack**, was the leader of Section 4.

As the formations moved out, problems developed. Ten planes would eventually return to North Africa due to mechanical problems. Over the Ionian Sea, just off the island of Corfu, **Wongo-Wongo**, lead aircraft of the Liberandos' second wave, had major problems and swiftly went out of control. As many flight crews watched, **Wongo-Wongo** began to wobble, dipped its nose first up then down, rolled over, and dove straight down into the sea. There were no survivors.

The morning wore on with the 376th and 93rd formations out in front. The weather over the Mediterranean was good. About noon however, as the planes approached land and the mountains of Albania and Yugoslavia, Col. Compton and General Ent, in the lead mission plane **Teggie Ann**, looked ahead and saw towering cloud formations reaching to 16,000 feet, or 6,000 feet higher than the planes' planned altitude. Since Compton had to clear the mountains and not lose any of his formation, and since his planes were equipped with oxygen, he took them up to 12,000 feet. They picked up a tail wind as they flew through gaps in the clouds in a long line of 3- and 4-plane elements. The 93rd followed suit. The remaining three squadrons, led by Col. Kane and maintaining a slower flying speed, fell behind.

By the time the three lagging bomb groups arrived at the cloud mass, they were about a mile below and 50-60 miles behind Compton and Ent. Few of Kane's planes carried oxygen, and since Kane wanted to both conserve fuel and clear the mountains, he led the formation straight into the clouds, flying on instruments. Pilots and co-pilots strained their eyes in case another plane came too close in the pea-soup denseness, but luckily there were no collisions. Shortly after 1100 hours they finally came out on the other side with all planes accounted for. They crossed the Danube River, entering air space over Romania. The crews had no idea what had happened to the 376th and 93rd.

Since radio silence was being observed, visual sighting was all the pilots had to go on. Even though the formations were now flying over Romania, no enemy aircraft were sighted. Everyone hoped they would achieve the surprise they wanted and, as the planes

106

came down to 1,000 feet, the prospects looked good. The pilots had no way of knowing that the mandatory radio silence had been useless. German encryption specialists had already broken the American military codes and knew that a large contingent of planes had left Libya in the early morning hours. The formation had also been spotted near Corfu and reported. A German radar installation near Sofia, Yugoslavia, had also picked up the lead formation and reported it to the German fighter defense headquarters in Bucharest. Sirens started sounding in Ploesti as the Germans and Romanians rushed to their defensive attack positions.

The three bomb groups led by the 98th continued on toward their respective targets. Sixty-five miles from Ploesti, they dropped to 500 feet. Then Jack Wood's 389th left the formation, turned north and headed for Campina, its assigned target. Kane's and Johnson's formations headed east, where they would shortly make a southerly turn toward Ploesti, as planned. The 376th and 93rd were still out of sight. What happened to these two formations would change the entire outcome of the mission. (See diagrams on pages 112 and 113.)

About an hour earlier, the leading 376th Liberandos had made a costly error. Compton and Ent had led the two bomb groups over the foothills of the Balkan Mountains at about 1,000 feet. Flying east and nearing Ploesti, the planes descended to 500 feet and powered up to over 180 miles per hour. Visibility was hampered by mist and light rain as the bombers sped along. When the rails of anticipated railroad tracks were seen, Col. Compton attempted to fix his position. He didn't want to overshoot the critical I.P. of the little town of Floresti, and since he was unable to see the steam and smokestacks of Ploesti's refineries anywhere on the immediate horizon, he took control of the formation and gave the order to turn south. Unfortunately, the tracks belonged to Targoviste, another small town about 13 miles before the correct I.P. of Floresti.

Captain Harold Wicklund, lead mission navigator on **Teggie Ann,** called up to Compton and Ent, telling them that they had turned too soon. He was ignored. Major Appold, flying a short distance behind the lead plane in **G.I. Ginnie**, believed what his navigator was saying and broke radio silence. Calling ahead, he yelled, "Wrong turn! Wrong turn!", but Compton and Ent did not change course. Ramsay Potts in the 93rd's lead plane piloted by Addison Baker shouted, "Not here! Mistake! Mistake!," but by then all the planes were headed south, and the two formations stayed together. In minutes they were on their way to Bucharest.

In no time the 376th and 93rd were spotted and reported to the fighter defense headquarters in Bucharest. Immediately the Romanian military sounded the alert and sent their fighter pilots into action. Finally Compton and Ent admitted their error when they saw the city of Bucharest emerging out of the mist. It was too late to salvage the original plan, so they decided to swing around and head toward Ploesti, coming in over the southern edge of the city, where German artillery was the heaviest.

When the Liberandos reached the outskirts, ground fire was so intense that they turned east and then north in order to wage an attack from another direction. As they flew closer to the main targets, however, there was so much artillery fire that Compton and Ent decided to bomb anything strategic they could find. The command channel was turned on and the announcement made: "Turn to 300 degrees. Pick targets of opportunity."

The planes of Baker's 93rd did not follow the 376th all the way to Ploesti. Not long after making the wrong turn, Col. Baker had spotted the stacks and steam of

Ploesti's refineries off to his left and gave the order to turn north. This maneuver led him and his planes straight for the target, right into the path of the heavily armed Germans who were waiting for them. Eight of the Flying Circus' 37 B-24s went down, torn apart by anti-aircraft fire. One more was shot down by an enemy fighter. Baker's plane, **Hell's Wench**, hit a barrage balloon and crashed in flames just past the target. The entire crew was killed. The remaining planes dropped their bombs on the Astra Romana, Unirea and Columbia Aquila refineries, then left. Unfortunately, these targets had been assigned to Kane's 98th and Johnson's 44th, who were fast approaching the target from the north at ground level. As the 93rd's remaining planes turned west heading home, they were on a collision course with the two incoming bomb groups.

One lone pilot of the 93rd, John Palm in **Brewery Wagon**, hadn't gone along with the turn toward Bucharest. Convinced the Flying Circus was headed on a wrong course, he broke away early and turned back toward Ploesti. Coming in low and apprehensive, he met with waiting German 88 mm anti-aircraft artillery. In the ensuing battle, **Brewery Wagon** took a deadly shell to the nose that instantly killed the bombardier and navigator. One engine was blown to pieces, two were on fire, and Palm's right leg was almost completely severed below the knee. He jettisoned his bombs and made a desperate crash-landing in an open field, thereby saving his life and the lives of the rest of his crew. The eight men were quickly captured, given first aid, and made prisoners-of-war.

Kane's Pyramidiers and Johnson's Flying 8-Balls were now coming in low and close together at full power, high RPM, and speeds of over 200 mph. There was no room to maneuver, and planes shuddered violently from severe prop wash. They were following their flight plan exactly, but the scenario had changed. When Col. Kane saw Ploesti coming up fast on the horizon, he couldn't understand why the sky was so dark. At first he thought it was a thunderstorm, then he realized it was black smoke from oil fires. Why were the refineries already burning?

The situation became critical as the planes quickly approached what was by now a blazing inferno. In addition to the dense smoke, the air was thickly peppered with flak as German anti-aircraft artillery were sending up 20-lb projectiles at a rate of 15 rounds per minute. As the men in the two formations braced themselves for the worst, fast command decisions had to be made.

To this day many people believe that Cols. Kane and Johnson should have turned back. The danger to bomb- and gas-laden planes flying into high-reaching flames, barrage balloons and billowing smoke at such low altitudes was enormous. The target had already been hit, but Kane was not about to be turned away from his long-prepared-for mission. The two commanders decided to press on as the B-24s turned toward the burning target.

By the time the planes of the 98th and 44th were just three minutes or 13 miles from the refineries, they had picked up a tail wind and were coming in fast. Practically scraping the ground, one plane was flying so low it sheared off the tops of trees. Others caught cornstalks in their open bomb bay doors. As they approached the target, the planes on the right side of the 98th flew directly over a fast-moving German train that was traveling in a straight line with the planes. As the box-car sides fell away, the American crews could see heavily manned anti-aircraft artillery that were so close that the men could look right into the deadly shiny barrels. This was the now-famous Q-train that was designed for just such a raid. The Germans opened full on the low-flying bombers, scoring many direct hits. Dozens of men were killed or wounded. Engines caught on fire. Controls were knocked out and fires erupted in cockpits and bomb bays.

Then, without warning, the errant planes of Baker's 93rd came through the smoke at right angles to Kane's group. The 98th pilots and other crew members who could see what was happening stared in disbelief at the B-24s flying directly above and below them. One pilot looked up and into the open bomb bay doors of another B-24. He could see the rows of bombs and half expected them to come down on his plane. Several Liberators from the 376th also came close to the cross-cutting planes, but managed to pull away. Amazingly, there were no collisions. Germans on the ground could not believe what they saw, and concluded that this near-miss must have been a brilliantly executed maneuver.

After their great scare and near misses, the 98th and 44th flew head-long into the darkness. Searing flames reaching hundreds of feet into the sky promptly wrapped themselves around fuselages and reached into open bomb bay doors. Oily black smoke enveloped the planes, giving the pilots zero visibility. There was often no way to see the tall refinery smokestacks that had to be cleared. Pilots powered up, praying they wouldn't hit anything. More than one banked around a smokestack; others weren't so lucky. Stacks 200 feet high were hit head-on and B-24s fell to the ground in flames. Other planes snagged one or more of the many steel barrage balloon cables that were rigged with bombs.

The cables ripped through fuselages and wings, often causing enough damage to bring down the plane. Major Bob Sternfels, piloting **Sandman**, took a shiny cable to the No. 3 propeller rather than let it take off a

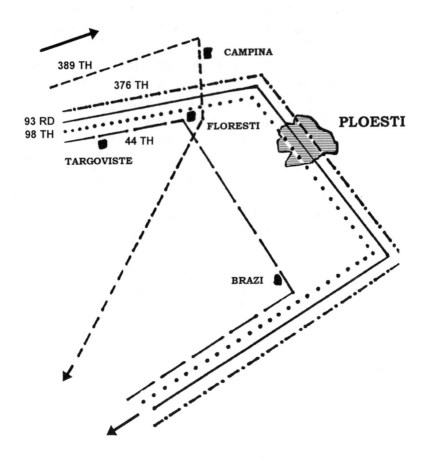

Figure 3. Ploesti bomb groups' planned flight paths.

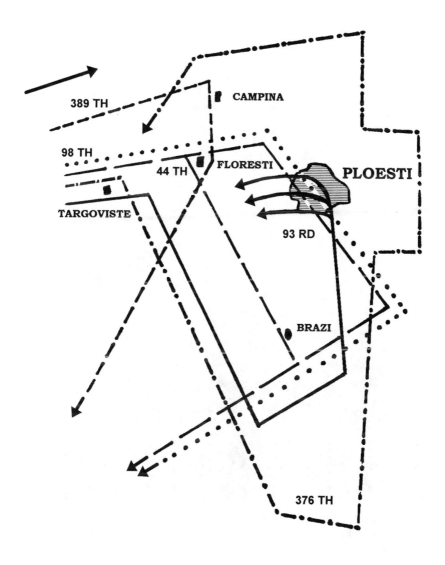

Figure 4. Ploesti bomb groups' actual flight paths.

Lil Jughaid, piloted by Robert Nicholson, and other B-24s from the 98th leaving the target low to the ground. Fire and smoke are from crashed B-24. (National Archives Still Pictures)

Oil storage tanks of Columbia Aquila refinery on fire as B-24s approach on their bomb run. (National Archives Still Pictures)

Close-up of Columbia Aquila's burning oil tanks and camouflage.
(National Archives Still Pictures)

wing or drag up a bomb. The cable was severed and the plane made it through the smoke in one piece.

The men fought back with all their might against the enemy ground fire, sometimes getting into one-on-one combat with a gunner firing from his land position. Nazi and Romanian fighters dipped through the smoke to take advantage of the handicapped Liberators that could not take evasive action. Several of the fighters flew too low and too fast and ended up crashing to earth because they could not pull up in time. Liberator gunners blasted away at the fighters from their precarious positions, hoping to rid the sky of at least one more German pilot. German fighter pilots would press their attack until they ran out of ammunition or fuel, or were shot down.

The American bombardiers let loose and dropped their bombs whenever they could. Anti-aircraft fire was tremendous. Few men in the B-24s thought they would get out alive as they employed every resource and ounce of strength to continue doing what was asked of them. Under the worst possible conditions, flight crews desperately fought fires in the cockpits and bellies of the planes. Those who could tried to aid the wounded. Faces and limbs were blown away. Many men continued to fight with dead comrades by their sides. Several co-pilots had to take over the controls because their pilot was either dead or wounded. Men were surrounded by leaking fuel and hydraulic fluid mixed with blood. Screams of pain rang out as crew members were hit by flak blasts.

The heat coming into the planes from the fires was almost unbearable, and trying to maintain controls or operate machine guns was next to impossible. Updrafts and down-drafts created severe turbulence, and it took all the strength the pilots had to keep the planes in the air. Gas tanks mounted in the bomb bays blew up. Ammunition boxes exploded. Burning and disintegrating B-24s could be seen streaking to the earth one after another. Gunners furiously worked their guns, hoping to knock out flak artillery or bring down German fighter pilots who were working just as hard to knock down the B-24s.

The mayhem over Ploesti seemed to go on forever, but in reality the entire attack took approximately one-half hour. The trusty Liberators, brutally damaged, gave safe haven to many crews. The death toll was high, however, as 35 planes with over 300 men onboard went down at or just past the target. It was such a nerve-shattering and horrifying experience that to this day many veterans of the mission cannot bear to talk about it.

Most of the B-24s that crashed in Romania were flaming fireballs. Several managed to skid to a stop in rural cornfields. Some lucky crew members walked away from their burning wreckage; most did not. The bodies of many of those killed were burned beyond recognition. Men who survived a crash were often burned and/or badly wounded. Most were rounded up by Romanians and Germans. Some were robbed and beaten; others were sent to hospitals and internment camps. A few were taken in by compassionate Romanians like Princess Catherine Caradja, who tried to keep them out of the hands of the Germans. Hundreds ended up being held as prisoners-of-war in Romania until the war ended.

Amazingly, many of the blackened, scorched and shot-up Liberators made it safely through to the other side of the inferno. **Maternity Ward** was one of them. After having dropped her bombs about 70-to-100 feet above the Astra Romana refinery, and after having suffered from the 93rd's bombs blowing up under the plane and attacks by German fighters, she was still aloft. It was shortly after 3:00 in the afternoon when the sand-colored B-24, with one engine out and its plexiglass nose full of holes, slowly gained altitude and turned back toward the Danube and North Africa.

Lt. Andrew L. Anderson, co-pilot of **Maternity Ward**, during flight training in October 1942.

Astra Romana refinery on fire during August 1, 1943 low-level raid. (National Archives Still Pictures)

Major Robert Sternfels' famous **Sandman** emerging from the eye of the Ploesti firestorm. Photo was taken by an automatic camera mounted in the tail of **Chug-a-Lug**, piloted by Captain LeRoy Morgan. (National Archives Still Pictures)

Sandman over Astra Romana refinery. (National Archives Still Pictures)

122

Sandman headed away from the target on the way out of enemy territory. Photo taken from tail of **Chug-a-Lug**. (USAAF photo as reprinted in August 1, 1943 newspaper)

Crew members and nose art of **Sandman**.

Standing L-R: pilot Robert W. Sternfels; co-pilot Barney Jackson; navigator Anthony Flesch; bombardier Dave Polaschek; flight engineer Bill Stout. Kneeling L-R: radio operator Frank Just; assistant radio operator and gunner Harry Rifkin; gunner Norbert Petri; gunner Merle Bolen; assistant flight engineer and gunner Ray Stewart. (Robert Sternfels)

10. TRYING TO GET BACK

Most of the noble Liberators that made it through the deadly raid and were trying to get back to North Africa were badly damaged. The pilots' job was to gain altitude, conserve fuel, and get out of enemy territory as quickly as possible. Squadron formations no longer existed, so it was every pilot for himself.

B-24s that could find each other joined up in an effort to provide some safety in numbers. Many engines were either inoperable or leaking oil. Some ships still carried bombs and other weight that slowed their progress. In many cases fuselages were full of holes and controls badly damaged. Inside, men were dead and wounded.

German pilots circling the area were eager to find crippled ships as they were easy prey. Before long Messerschmitt ME-109s and Focke Wulf FW-190s descended like hawks, trying to knock the damaged planes out of the sky. More B-24s went down. Some men managed to survive their crashed plane, many more were killed. A significant number parachuted to safety. Plans had been in place for a long time as to what to do if one found himself in Romania. Each carried Romanian money, maps, compasses, and other survival essentials.

Maternity Ward finally cleared land and headed out to sea. The nervous crew, with pilot John Ward and co-pilot Andrew Anderson carefully working the controls, flew along the coast of Greece and turned south at Corfu. **Maternity Ward** had linked up with another damaged ship, Ned McCarty's **Cornhusker**, so there was hope. Going was slow, and although the two ships were about five miles behind a nine-plane formation with whom they had radio contact, they flew doggedly forward over the shining water. What was about to happen, however, was later referred to as the "Ionian Sea ambush."

B-24, in trouble, trying to get back to base.
(National Archives Still Pictures)

11. *MATERNITY WARD* GOES DOWN

The lead ship of the nine-plane formation ahead radioed that they would slow down to let the two stragglers catch up. Everything seemed to be going smoothly. Then the German fighters appeared. Usually the fighters turned back when they reached the coastline, but this time they gave full pursuit. Six FW-190s and two ME-109s came right for the two planes, guns ablaze. Lt. Crump took out one of the fighters, but it wasn't enough. Their companion ship, **Cornhusker**, went down with two smoking engines and hit the water hard. Ward and his crew were left alone.

The Germans pursued **Maternity Ward** relentlessly. Coming up from the rear, they shot out the tail turret, and wounded Sgt. Long. As he screamed for help, cannon and machine-gun fire came in from the back of the plane and went clear through to the front. The tail was destroyed and the elevator cables severed, and there was fire in the bomb bay gas tank. Sgt. Pemberton was also wounded, but even so he wanted to make his way through the fire and try to help in the rear of the ship. Lt. Anderson told him to stay where he was as the fire was too severe. The plane was in bad shape. The hydraulic system was gone, along with the communications system. The plane quickly went out of control and into a steep dive.

Ward eased back on the throttle and tried to lower the flaps to slow the plane down. The flaps were stuck, however, and the cut in power resulted in only increasing the diving angle. Lt. Anderson, who had taken some shrapnel, left the cockpit to try to fight the fire in the bomb bay as the plane swiftly lost altitude. Nothing was heard from the other crew members.

As a last-ditch effort, Ward added power. The fire in the bomb bay was spreading rapidly. Anticipating an explosion before the plane hit the water, he tried to bring the plane under control. The bell alarm signal was given to abandon ship, but there was no way of knowing whether any of the crew members in the back of the ship heard it. The flight home was over-- **Maternity Ward** was finished.

After significantly leveling the plane, Lt. Ward left the cockpit and discovered that Sgt. Pemberton's parachute had been shattered by cannon fire. Neither Pemberton nor Sgt. Long, both of whom were wounded, could get out safely. It was Ward's and Anderson's decision to stay with the plane and try to ease the crash as much as possible by continuing to fight the fire and keeping the wings level. It was believed that Sgt. Turner had already gone out through the burning bomb bays.

Maternity Ward came down the final 3,000 feet at 240 mph, descending at 500-600 feet per minute. Since this was no longer an extremely steep dive, the rest of the crew members had time to get out if they were able or prepare themselves for the crash. Ward returned to the pilot's seat, neglecting to fasten his seat belt. Sgt. Pemberton opened the top hatch and braced himself against the armor plate behind Lt. Ward's seat, and Lt. Anderson pulled the dinghy release then braced himself against the other armor plate. The last thing Lt. Ward saw was the water rushing up to meet them.

After the plane hit the water, the nose broke away from the fuselage, and Ward was thrown clear. The waist and bomb bay burst into flames, and **Maternity Ward** began to sink tail first, nose up. Lts. Ward and Anderson briefly lost consciousness, then came to underwater and swam to the surface. Ward emerged about 50 feet away from one of the plane's wings, which had also broken off from the fuselage and was floating, trailing edge up. In a short time the entire wreckage sank.

When Lt. Anderson regained consciousness he was still in the pilot's compartment that was rapidly sinking. He felt around for Pemberton and found him, but he was trapped by the top turret, which had broken loose. There was no way Anderson could free him. To save himself, he went up through the hatch opening while choking and swallowing water. Surfacing in the middle of burning gasoline, he dove and swam underwater until he came up free of the flames.

Ward was swimming around furiously, looking for any other sign of life when miraculously, Lt. Anderson came to the surface about 50 feet away. Ward yelled at him, and within a few minutes they were swimming side-by-side. They grabbed on to some floating oxygen tanks and hung on until about five minutes later a life raft came up and they were able to climb aboard. Anderson told Ward about Pemberton who was trapped in the wreckage. This brave man, who struggled so valiantly in spite of his wounds, had drowned.

Ward and Anderson, badly shaken, tried to assess their situation. They knew they were adrift somewhere between Italy and Greece. Anderson, who had swallowed much sea water and inhaled noxious fumes from the burning fuel, vomited again and again. Apart from the sounds being made by the two men, the sea was deadly quiet as the afternoon slowly faded into evening. In one last effort to locate any more survivors, the two men rowed back along the flight line, calling until they were hoarse. No one answered. Finally, exhausted, they greeted the night sitting in three inches of water and shivering. It was next to impossible to get any sleep as the night air grew colder and their clothing consisted of underwear, socks, khaki shorts and short-sleeved shirts.

As the morning light broke and the sun appeared, the two weary men looked over their survival kits that had surfaced with the life rafts. The water cans were broken open, and the "D" bars were badly soaked. The flares and matches were wet. They had little food and no water, and no way to rig a sail. They knew their fate was to drift with the current, hoping someone would come looking for them.

For the next two days they sat in their wet raft, baking in the hot sun, waiting for something to happen. At night they laid in the bottom of the raft, arms wrapped around each other for body warmth. Ward drove Anderson nearly crazy because he constantly cleared his parched throat. In the still of the night, the sound was almost unbearable.

Then, on the third night, rescue came so close that it seemed like a dream. A beautifully lit ship came right for them but turned away as they struggled to light their wet flares. As the third flare finally fired and lit up the raft, voices of men running on the decks could be heard. Ward and Anderson yelled as loud as they could, but the noise of the ship's engines drowned them out. They didn't know if anyone had seen them. As they watched the ship's lights fade out of sight, their hearts sank. They watched and waited in case someone came back, but no one did.

After five more days and nights of searing heat and bitter cold, the two men dreamt about food and drink. It was a startling event, therefore, when a scrawny albatross made a crash landing in the raft, ending up on Anderson's shoulder. Ward made a giant leap from one end of the raft to the other and grabbed the bird, glad for the food that had dropped like manna from the heavens. But Anderson wasn't so sure. Feeling sorry for the bedraggled thing with the scared eyes, he held it for a while then let it go. If Ward weren't so weak, he would have gone after Anderson with a vengeance and tried to wring *his* neck.

As one miserable day drifted into another, the two men thought often of just jumping overboard and ending it all. Their mouths were dry and cracked. Their hands, feet, lips and tongue were swollen and painful, and their wounds festered and broke. The sun beat relentlessly during the day; the nights were dark and cold. These brave airmen cried as they prayed for someone to find them, but their prayers appeared to be in vain.

Finally, on day twelve, two British *Beaufighters* spotted them and signaled that they would send a rescue team. Ward and Anderson collapsed on the bottom of the raft with joy. All night they stayed awake waiting for a boat, a plane, anything. As dawn broke on the thirteenth day they saw it—a powerboat going fast through the water. Frantically they waved and yelled. They threw their shirts and pants up in the air, but the boat crew never saw them and sped away. Incredible. A second near-rescue, and now total despair.

The rest of the day, starving and dehydrated, John Ward and Andrew Anderson stared at the blurry horizon as if in a trance, weak and close to delirium. Then, when the mist lifted for a few minutes, they thought they must be hallucinating for something that looked like land appeared then faded away. With great effort they took the oars and started rowing. They rowed day and night toward the apparition.

On August 16, after fifteen full days at sea, they came to within 300 yards of a small island, but it had no beach on which to land the raft. About half a mile away was another island, so they decided to try to make it there. Finally, when they were close enough to go ashore, they heaved themselves overboard. The water was only waist-deep, but they had great difficulty staying on their feet. In a last desperate effort they crawled on their hands and knees until they fell exhausted on the beach. The pilot and co-pilot of **Maternity Ward** had finally made a safe landing.

As they laid on the beach they heard an unbelievable sound: singing! They rose to their knees in disbelief as a boatload of Italian soldiers landed, came over and picked them up, then gently laid them in their boat. After rowing to a nearby sheltered harbor, they carried Anderson and Ward to a building near an old castle and gave them food and water. The two men were put in beds and a doctor came to tend their wounds.

The island where the two men landed was the Greek island of Kithera, that was occupied by the Italian military and contained a German garrison. The Italian soldiers allowed people from nearby villages to visit the two prisoners, which helped Ward and Anderson recover. Fresh fruit, bread and wine became their daily sustenance, and medical help included ointment for their severe sunburn. They were given haircuts and shaves as the dead skin on their hands, faces, feet and legs began to peel off.

Eventually they were allowed to exercise in the courtyard, which included jumping over two empty graves that had been dug for them, and visit with the Italian guards. Some of the guards were very friendly and declared they were unhappy to be in the war and were waiting for it to end. They planned to escape to the hills when Italy surrendered and wait for the Allies to land. Ward and Anderson planned to go with them.

One month later in September, however, Italy capitulated to Germany, and the guards went nuts with disgust. They piled their guns and ammunition in the courtyard, doused them with kerosene, and lit a huge and dangerous bonfire that exploded well into the night. The two Americans hid behind a wall as the Italians got roaring drunk and sang for what seemed the entire night. Ward and Anderson could not escape to the hills because the bonfire blocked their exit route.

The next morning the Germans arrived and promptly took the two prisoners to a nearby radar site where they were put under lock and key for three days. A Fokker tri-plane equipped for water landings picked them up and flew them to Athens, where they were transferred to a car and driven to Salonika, Greece. There they were given captured English uniforms and put on a train to Frankfurt. In Frankfurt they were routed to a prisoner-of-war camp, Stalag Luft III, in Sagan, Germany.

For the next two years, the two valiant **Maternity Ward** officers lived through every kind of hardship associated with P.O.W. camps: sickness, hunger, freezing marches in the dead of winter, threats, bombings, fear and anxiety. The strength of these two men endured, however, and in 1945 when Allied forces invaded Germany and liberated the camps, Lt. John Vernon Ward and Lt. Andrew L. Anderson were free men. Within weeks they set foot once again on American soil.

Andrew Anderson and another American serviceman in German prison camp Stalag Luft III, 1944.

Goodnight, sweet prince.

From a 1943 issue of the 98th Bomb Group's magazine:

*To those members of the Squadron who, in recent
weeks, failed to return from their missions.
They went down in the finest traditions of
the Air Corps, maintaining their guns to the last.
We shall miss them, but they are an inspiration
to us, for in their gallant conduct, they have set an
example for everyone of the Air and Ground Echelon.*

EPILOGUE

Bill Fay was never heard from again. Of the 1,735 crew members and 178 B-24s that took off from Benghazi in the early morning hours of August 1, 1943, 54 planes were lost and over 300 crew members were killed. Close to 200 were held prisoner in Romania. Gunners from the 98th destroyed 36 enemy planes, but this heroic attempt to bomb Ploesti cost them dearly in aircraft and crew.

Of the 98th Bomb Group's 48 aircraft: 8 turned back before reaching the target area; 1 was lost before reaching the target; 14 went down at or near the target; 6 were lost after leaving the target area; 6 were diverted to an allied base after the raid; and 13 returned safely to base in North Africa. Close to half of the 98th was gone forever: 21 planes were lost and approximately 185 men were killed-in-action, wounded, or held as prisoner-of-war. Regarding the mission, both the United States and Germany claimed victory.

It was reported that 50% or more of oil production at Ploesti was destroyed as a result of the raid. Germany's war machine was slowed down for a while, and the mission declared a success. Of the seven refinery complexes, two were heavily damaged, two had light damage, two were shut down for six months, and one was left intact. In less than two months, most of the damaged refineries were back in production. It took one more year before Ploesti's refineries were totally destroyed as a result of numerous Allied bomb attacks. Shortly thereafter the city fell to advancing Russian troops who had driven out the Germans.

EXCERPT FROM DAVID GANDIN'S DIARY, August 1, 1943:

"Our squadron is no more. Missing and probably killed in action are Dore, Finneran, Franks, Stallings, Fay, Howie, Sulflow, Schlenker, Shay, Miller, Deeds, Crump, Foster, Scarborough, Ward, Huntly, Money, Anderson, Hussey, Peterson, Dave Lewis, Jenkins, Nelson, Thomas, Nash, McCandless, plus all of their enlisted men. I hope the price was worth it. They're the finest fellows in the world."

AUTHOR'S NOTE:

Regarding the above-mentioned crew members, the following statistics apply:

Maternity Ward
Survived: Andrew Anderson (CP), John Ward (P)
Killed in Action: Henry C. Crump, Jr., (B), William Fay (G), Beverly Huntley (N)

Kate Smith
P.O.W.-Romania: Clifton Foster (CP)
Killed in Action: James Deeds (P), Theodore Scarborough (B)

Old Baldy
Killed in Action: John Dore, Jr. (P), Joseph Finneran (B), Worthington Franks (N), John Stallings (CP) (see crew photo, page 27)

Cornhusker
Killed in Action: Clyde Miller (CP)

Lil Joe
P.O.W.-Romania: Lindley Hussey (P)
Killed in Action: Donald Jenkins (CP), Phillip Nelson (N),
Allan Peterson (B)

Aire Lobe
Killed in Action: David Lewis (CP, George McCandless
(B), Robert Nash (N), John Thomas (P)

Semper Felix
Killed in Action: Leroy Schlenker (CP), Phillip Miller (N),
Arnel Shay, Jr. (B), August Sulflow (P)

Money and Howie could not be located.

BILL FAY'S CREW

Bill Fay's crew and two former planes fared as follows:
Captain Wes Egan, still suffering from the effects of
sand fly fever, was not allowed to take his plane or crew
on the Ploesti mission, even though those with 300 hrs
flying time were being kept in North Africa for the low-
level attack. Except for Bill Fay, the crew stayed on the
ground and left the next day for the U.S.A.

Lil Joe, piloted by Lindley Hussey, went on the mission
and crashed in Romania. Most of the crew bailed out,
but the plane was close to the ground and not everyone
survived. Four crew members, including Hussey, the
radio operator Edmond Terry, the waist gunner
Raymond Heisner, and a second gunner James Turner
survived and were held as P.O.W.s in Romania. The
other five crew members were killed.

Li'l De-Icer, patched almost beyond recognition, flew
with pilot James Merrick and returned safely.

Prisoners-Of-War after their release from Romanian camps in 1944.
(National Archives Still Pictures)

Liberated American airmen on their way home from Romanian prison camps in 1944. (National Archives Still Pictures)

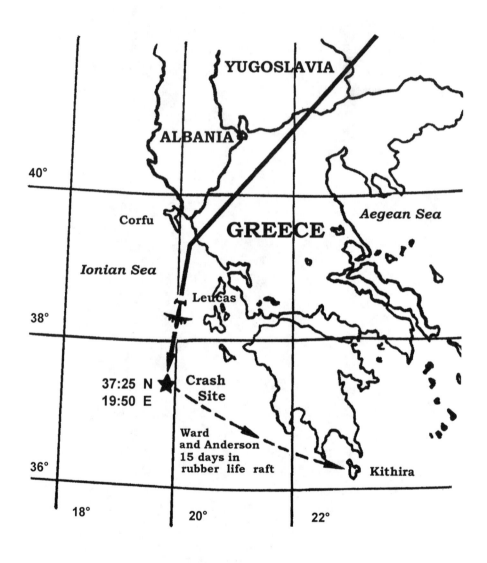

Figure 5. Crash site of **Cornhusker** and **Maternity Ward**,
August 1, 1943.

APPENDIX A.
SITE OF THE CRASH

Two B-24 pilots flying back to North Africa on August 1, 1943, filed sortie reports in which they described seeing two planes hit the water off the coast of Greece. The author believes these planes were **Cornhusker** and **Maternity Ward**. Both pilots, 1st Lt. LeRoy B. Morgan of **Chug-A-Lug** and Flight Officer Charles A. Salyer of **Battle Axe**, reported seeing four parachutes exit a pink B-24 that could have been **Maternity Ward**.

One of the four parachutes probably belonged to Sgt. Turner, who was believed to have gone out through the bomb bays. Another could have been worn by Lt. Huntley, who was reported killed in action a year later. That left two more parachutes reported and five crew members unaccounted for: Crum (bombardier), Toth (top turret gunner), Scott (gunner), Long (tail gunner who was wounded), and Fay (waist gunner). It is possible that Toth exited the top turret.

Any other men who made it out before the plane hit the water could have been picked up by a friendly fishing craft or a German ship, attacked by barracuda, or drowned. As we know, no one answered Ward's and Anderson's calls as they paddled back along the flight path. Those who went down with the plane were most likely killed by gunfire or by the explosion and subsequent sinking.

The author believes that the two sortie reports establish the crash site of **Cornhusker** and **Maternity Ward.** Information and data taken from these sortie reports is as follows. Items in parentheses are comments by the author.

SORTIE REPORT NO. 1

Filed by pilot 1ˢᵗ Lt. LeRoy B. Morgan, flying **Chug-a-Lug**, dated August 1, 1943:

Time: 18:45
Place: 37:25N, 19:50E
Narrative:
One B-24, pink, slid down gradually from behind and to our left, trailing white smoke. It hit the water and burned with a red flame. One wing staid [sic] afloat a long while. Six chutes were seen to open; a seventh man jumped and hit the water. [This is believed to be the plane **Cornhusker**.]

At the same spot a second pink B-24 hit the water to our right. One engine was feathered; four chutes were seen to open. Both these ships were brought down by pursuit. [This is believed to be the plane **Maternity Ward**.]

SORTIE REPORT NO. 2

Filed by pilot F/O Charles A. Salyer, flying **Battle Axe**, dated August 1, 1943:

Time: 18:30
Place: none given
Narrative:
Pursuit waiting for us in sun off Leukas shot down one pink B-24 straggling well below us and to right rear. He turned on his left wing and hit the water in a long streamer of flame. 1-2 parachutes opened. [This is believed to be the plane **Cornhusker** even though there is a disparity in number of parachutes.]

Just after a second pink B-24 low, behind to our left had #3 engine on fire. It was loosing [sic] altitude fast; as it hit the waist and bomb bay burst into flame and the plane sank tail first, nose up after several minutes.

Saw four parachutes. [This is believed to be the plane **Maternity Ward**].

PILOT JOHN WARD'S REPORT

In the "Report of Lt. John Ward," the pilot of **Maternity Ward**, to families of missing crew members dated August 1, 1945, the following is stated:

Maternity Ward along with another damaged Liberator was unable to climb as rapidly as the other ships.... As we were crossing the coast and heading out to sea we were intercepted by fighters....A half dozen FW-190's and a couple of ME-109's headed directly for us. ...our companion ship was shot down. ...[enemy fire] started a fire in the bomb bay gas tank...Sgt. Turner had...jumped. We descended...3000 feet at an average descent of five or six hundred feet per minute at the speed of over 200 miles per hour.

BOOK REFERENCE OF SIGHTING

In Michael Hill's book, *Black Sunday: Ploesti*, Hill states that **Cornhusker**, piloted by Ned McCarty, crashed at a position of 37:53N, 20:13E off the coast of Greece. This is the area of the "Ionian Sea Ambush."

The almost identical coordinates given in Sortie Report No. 1 (37:25N, 19:50E) and the close time factors of 18:45 and 18:30 given in Sortie Reports Nos. 1 and 2 make a strong case for **Cornhusker** and **Maternity Ward** going down as indicated in the diagram on page 140.

Big guns on rails found near the Ploesti refineries in 1944. (National Archives Still Pictures)

144

APPENDIX B. CORRESPONDENCE WITH MARIE FAY, BILL'S SISTER, AND OFFICIAL NOTICE

Letter from Ethel M. Scott, mother of S/Sgt. Harold W. Scott dated January 5, 1944:

Dear Miss Fay,

I am the mother of S/Sgt. Scott...your brother was on the same bomber with my son. Is your brother missing,...do you have any information about him or the crew? It is such a heartbreaking experience.

Letter from Thelma Pace, mother of S/Sgt. Robert E. Long dated January 3, 1944:

My dear Miss Fay:

I am the mother of Robert Long, tail gunner on the "Maternity Ward." On August 13th I was notified my son was missing in action. Was your brother on the **Maternity Ward**? Did you hear that the pilot and co-pilot are German prisoners? I assume if the pilots got out then the rest did too. Please write to me and any more news I hear I will send to you.

Letter from Mrs. Marie Turner, sister-in-law of S/Sgt. Kenneth L. Turner, dated January 3, 1944:

My dear Miss Fay:

My father-in-law, Tilford Turner, whose son Kenneth is missing, is unable to write at the present time so I am writing for him.

At the present time there has been no word of Kenneth or any of the crew that we know of. Kenneth's father has had to see the parting of so many of his sons, relatives and friends, and we'd all be very thankful if you would write if you could tell us any information you might receive.

Letter from Leon Pemberton, Sr., father of T/Sgt. Leon D. Pemberton, dated December 31, 1943:

Dear Miss Fay:

I am the father of T/Sgt. Leon D. Pemberton who was a member of the crew on the plane which is missing in action on which your brother was an engineer. I would like to learn definitely whether it is possible that my son may be a prisoner of war or whether there is a chance that he came out of this raid alive. Should you have any information concerning the raid I would appreciate hearing from you and I will be glad to give you any information which I may have or may secure in the future concerning any of the boys.

Letter from T/Sgt. Byron Chiverton (no date given):

Dear Miss Fay:

I really don't know how to write this letter as I have the words in me but really don't know how to say them.

I know by now you know of Bill being among the missing on the Romanian oil field raid. But before I go further, I was on the same crew as Bill. We flew, ate, worked, played and slept and lived together every day for over a year, and I considered Bill a brother of mine and I am very proud of him.

I myself believe Bill is still alive but is a prisoner or is on the loose in Europe someplace as there were many fellows who went down on that mission but have been showing up every now and then. I've prayed for him coming out of it so many times that I know his is OK.

There were only five of us who did come out without a scratch and we arrived back in the States about one and one-half months ago.

Bill was laid up with malaria for about a week and the rest of us finished up our amount of combat hours before him. So it was on his last mission with another crew that he went down.

I have a few of his things at home which I will send you. I imagine you received some pictures of his that the censor took from me. One of the things being sent is the Distinguished Flying Cross which you should be very proud of because he earned it by saving our ship once when we were being attacked by enemy fighters and also by saving my life when I passed out from lack of oxygen. Also there is the air medal (ribbon) which he received for 100 hrs combat, and his European Theatre ribbon. All we have to do is hope and pray for his safe return.

Letter from T/Sgt. Byron Chiverton (no date given):

Dear Miss Fay:

I wrote home the other day and gave my folks the word to send Bill's things to you. I was wondering if you received a bunch of pictures from the censors because they are really good pictures.

Well, guess I'll have to run now so will close. If you write you don't have to call me T/Sgt. Chiverton. Bill called me Pop.

Sincerely, Pop

Byron Chiverton, November 18, 1942,
Gunnery School, Topeka, Kansas

STANDARD TIME INDICATED
RECEIVED AT

TELEPHONE YOUR TELEGRAMS TO POSTAL TELEGRAPH

M. CB372   C. WA287   1943 AUG 13 PM 4 56

WMUA 43 47 GOVT=WMU WASHINGTON DC AUG 13 411P=:

MISS MARIE T FAY =

1136 JOHNSON STREET NORTHEAST MINNEAPOLIS MINN

I REGRET TO INFORM YOU REPORT RECEIVED STATES YOUR BROTHER
STAFF SERGEANT WILLIAM J FAY MISSING IN ACTION IN MIDDLE
EASTERN AREA SINCE ONE AUGUST IF FURTHER DETAILS OR OTHER
INFORMATION OF HIS STATUS ARE RECEIVED YOU WILL BE PROMPTLY
NOTIFIED==

        ULIO THE ADJUTANT GENERAL 424P =(

:ONF MISS MARIE T FAY 1136 WILLIAM J

Telegram dated August 13, 1943

Mission accomplished, and now to get home.
(National Archives Still Pictures)

APPENDIX C.
AWARDS AND
CITATION OF HONOR

Bill Fay received the following awards during his brief time in the United States Army Air Forces:

- *Distinguished Flying Cross*
- *Distinguished Flying Cross With Oak Leaf Cluster*
- *Purple Heart*
- *European Theatre Ribbon*
- *Air Medal*

In addition, he was given the *Citation of Honor,* the text of which follows:

> *He lived to bear his country's arms. He died to save its honor. He was a soldier...and he knew a soldier's duty. His sacrifice will help to keep aglow the flaming torch that lights our lives... that millions yet unborn may know the priceless joy of liberty. And we who pay him homage, and revere his memory, in solemn pride rededicate ourselves to a complete fulfillment of the task for which he so gallantly has placed his life upon the altar of man's freedom.*

BIBLIOGRAPHY

BOOKS

Adlen, Robert N., *In the Lion's Mouth*, based on the diary of Captain David Gandin, Emis Publishing Co., Canoga Park, CA, 1987

Bailey, Ronald H., *The Air War in Europe*, Time-Life Books, Inc., Alexandria, VA, 1979

Craven, Wesley F. and Cate, James L., Ed., *The Army Air Forces in World War II, Vol. 2, Europe: Torch to Pointblank, August 1942 to December 1943*, The University of Chicago Press, Chicago, IL, 1956

Birdsall, Steve, *Log of the Liberators: An Illustrated History of the B-24*, Doubleday & Co., Inc., Garden City, N.Y., 1973

Davis, Larry, *B-24 Liberator in Action, Aircraft No. 80*, Squadron/Signal Publ., Inc., Carrolton, TX, 1987

Dugan, James and Stewart, Carroll, *Ploesti*, Random House, New York, NY, 1962

Force for Freedom, The Legacy of the 98th, Vol. II, "Fifteen Days Is a Long Time" by Andrew Anderson, Turner Publishing, Paducah, KY, 1990

Hill, Michael, *Black Sunday: Ploesti*, Schiffer Publishing, Ltd., Atglen, PA, 1993

Lee, David, *World War II Airplanes*, Chartwell Books, Inc., Edison, NJ, 1998

Newby, Leroy W., *Target Ploesti: A View from a Bombsight*, Presidio Press, Novato, CA 1983

Nickerson, Jane Soames, *A Short History of North Africa*, The Devin-Adair Company, New York, NY, 1961

The Oxford Companion to World War II, Oxford University Press, Oxford, NY, 1995

Sanders, Renfield, *Libya*, Chelsea House Publishers, 1987

Story of the 98th, The Pyramidiers, 1942-1945, George Baroni, Ed.

Walker, James W., *The Liberandos*, 376th Heavy Bombardment Group Veterans Association, Inc., 1994

Wolff, Leon, *Low Level Mission*, Doubleday and Co., Inc., Garden City, NY, 1957

MAGAZINES AND ARTICLES

Anderson, Andrew L., "Fifteen Days Is a Long Time," *Through the Eye of the Needle*, Stalag Luft III Former Prisoners of War, Gateway Press, Baltimore, MD, 1992

Frisbee, John L., "The Ordeal of **Sad Sack II**," *Air Force Magazine*, December 1994

O'Grady, John E., "Ploesti—August 1, 1943," *J. Second Air Division Association*, Vol. 29, No. 3, Fall 1990

O'Grady, John E., "Test Flight of B-24 Kate Smith," *J. Second Air Division Association*, Vol. 27, No. 4, Winter 1988

"Operation Torch: America's Four-Day War with France," *VFW Magazine*, November 1992

Opsata, Andrew, "Flight Over Ploesti," Parts 1 and 2 (unpublished)

Sternfels, Robert W., "Bomb Run, Low Level Mission to Ploesti Oil Refineries" (unpublished)

"Weatherwise," Helen Dwight Reid *Educational Foundation*, Vol. 48, Issue 3, June/July 1995

Whalen, Norman M., "Ploesti: Group Navigator's Eye View," *Aerospace Historian*, Spring (March) 1976

VIDEO PRESENTATIONS

"Air Combat II, Combat Crew", U.S. News Productions

"Ploesti! B-24 at War", American Sound & Video Corporation, 1990

"World War II With Walter Cronkite, Air War Over Europe", CBS Inc., 1983

LETTERS AND REPORTS

Report of Lt. John V. Ward to families of crew members, August 1945

Sortie Report filed by Flight Officer Charles A. Salyer, USAAF, Benina Main Airdrome, North Africa, August 1,1943

Sortie Report filed by 1/Lt. LeRoy B. Morgan, USAAF, Benina Main Airdrome, North Africa, August 1, 1943

INTERVIEWS

With Grover (Goady) A. Zink (Navigator) and Harold F. Weir (engineer/gunner) who flew on the B-24 **Squaw** in the August 1, 1943, low-level attack on Ploesti. 98th Bomb Group Reunion, Branson, MO., October 1997

Top: Harold and Betty Weir in 1997 and Harold as waist-gunner in 1943. Bottom: Navigator Grover (Goady) Zink in 1943 and Goady and LuHelen Zink in 1997.

ACKNOWLEDGEMENTS

All photos, except where given specific credit, were the property of Bill Fay and most probably taken by a U.S. Army Air Forces photographer.

I wish to thank the following people for their help and support:

Frederick Aronowitz; Pamela Madison DeMarais; Albert E. Madison, Jr.; William M. Madison; Donna Carlson Doering; William Whitney; Peter Frizzell; Timothy and Rachel Fahey; Ben Cottone; the family of Andrew L. Anderson, especially his son Myles and wife Patricia; and Susan Witt and Professor Michael J. Polay of Embry-Riddle Aeronautical University, Prescott, Arizona.

A special thanks to the members of the 98th Bomb Group--especially Secretary Stan Flentje; Art Plouff, ground maintenance man for the 98th during the Ploesti raid; Grover "Goady" Zink and Harold Weir who flew as navigator and waist-gunner on **Squaw**; Robert Sternfels who piloted **Sandman**; Roy Newton who flew as waist-gunner on **Hadley's Harem**; Andy Opsata who piloted **Stinger**; Wes Egan who commanded the crew of **Lil Joe** and **Li'l De-Icer**; John Matheson, who was Bill Fay's crew mate from basic training days up to August 1, 1943; and John Ward, who piloted the ill-fated **Maternity Ward**.

Marguerite Madison Aronowitz

GLOSSARY

Ack-ack. 88 mm anti-aircraft artillery mounted in fixed placements.

Beaufighter. The British Beaufighter was a twin-engined, two-crew night fighter and anti-shipping strike aircraft. It carried four 20 mm Hispano cannon, six 0.303-in. Browning machine guns, one 0.303-in. Vickers machine gun, and a combination of torpedo, rockets, and bombs when in anti-shipping role. Number built: 5918

Falouka. Small sailboat used on the waterways of Egypt.

Flak. Taken from the German word *Flugzeugabwehrkannon* (anti-aircraft gun). An explosive or fragmenting projectile resulting from the firing of loaded flak guns.

FW-190. The German Focke-Wulf FW-190 single-seat fighter was one of the principal defensive fighters against American bombing of German targets in World War II. It carried two 7.9 mm machine guns and four 20 mm cannon. Number built: 19500+.

Incendiaries ("cindies"). Explosives dropped from aircraft (usually by hand) to cause new fires or increase the flammability of something already burning.

I.P. Initial or identification point.

Jig-jig run. In this particular case, when a B-24 that belonged to the 98th and was stripped of all armaments flew to Cairo for supplies.

K.P. Kitchen police. Assignment to K.P. was and is not considered prestigious or desirable.

Kiwis. Term used to describe New Zealanders.

L.G. 159, etc. Terminology describing location of U.S. military posts in the North African desert.

Limeys. Term used to describe the British.

Lister bag. Large canvas water bag, holding approximately 35 gallons. Usually hung from a tree or pole when filled with water. Water was dispensed from multiple (6) spigots.

ME-109. The German Messerschmitt FW-190 single-seat fighter was built in greater numbers than any other fighter aircraft in World War II. It carried three 20 mm cannon and two 7.9 mm machine guns. Number built: 30500+.

ME-110. The German Messerschmitt ME-110 was a long-range, two- or three-crew, day-and-night fighter. It carried two 20 mm cannon and four 7.9 mm machine guns. Number built: 6000.

Pom-pom. 35 mm anti-aircraft guns. Used for shooting at individual targets, as opposed to guns used to generate large amounts of flak for penetrating plane fuselages. Often found in "flak towers".

Shrapnel. Pieces of metal from exploding shells that deeply imbed themselves as a result of the force of an explosion. Name comes from General H. Shrapnel of the British army.

Snaddey bomb. Small German explosive.

Spam. Canned meat product made by the Hormel Foods Corporation, that was distributed during World War II as a staple food product for the troops. Because of its extensive use and the varied ways in which it was prepared, it was often the butt of jokes. Spam may still be purchased in stores today.

Stuka. The German Junkers JU 87 Stuka was a two-seat dive bomber that made a distinctive shrieking sound when it went into a dive. The Stuka carried two fixed 7.9 mm machine guns, one flexible 7.9 mm machine gun, and a maximum bomb load of 1,100 pounds. It was mainly used as an air-ground support aircraft and did not fare well in air-to-air combat. Number built: 5700+.

Wimpy. The British Vickers Wellington six-crew medium bomber was known as the "Wimpy". This slow-moving plane featured unusual geodetic construction, had in-line engines, and carried six 0.303-in. machine guns and a maximum bomb load of 4500 pounds. Number built: 11460+.

INDEX

161

162

Bill Fay was born on April 11, 1921, in Minneapolis, Minnesota. His mother was Evelyn Madison Fahey, and his father was Edward Joseph Fahey. He attended Marshall High School in Southeast Minneapolis where, in his senior year, he won the state amateur wrestling championship for his weight. He had one sister, Marie, who died in 1992.

On July 5, 1942, at age 21, Bill enlisted in the United States Army Air Forces. He attended aerial gunnery school in Harlingen, Texas, after which he flew to Topeka, Kansas, where he teamed up with Lt. Wes Egan and the other crew members who flew together until the last weeks before Ploesti.

164

National Archives Photograph Numbers

The following photographs may be found at the National Archives, Still Pictures Division, 8601 Adelphi Road, College Park, Maryland 20740-6001.

Page 20: 342-FH-3A26156-55221; Page 21: 342-FH-3A26795-52520; Page 54: 342-FH-3A26842-55232; Page 99: 342-FH-3A26832-53121; Page 114: 342-FH-3A22498-24619; Page 115: 342-FH-3A26903-24640; Page 116: 342-FH-3A26900-24621; Page 120: 342-FH-3A26902-24621; Page 121: 342-FH-3A26824-25157; Page 122: 342-FH-3A26901-24621; Page 126: 342-FH-3A26567-12348; Page 138: 342-FH-3A24222-54092; Page 139: 342-FH-3A24221-54091; Page 144: 342-FH-3A26779-55240; Page 150: 342-FH-3A26802-50796.

Order Form

To order additional copies of this book, send check or money order for $14.95 per book, plus postage and handling to:

> Pine Castle Books
> P.O. Box 4397
> Prescott, AZ, 86302-4397

_____ books at $14.95 $_____

AZ residents add 5.5% sales tax   _____
  ($.82 per book)

Postage and handling
  ($3.00 for first book, $.75
  for each additional book)   _____

                    Total due $_____

Please allow 4-6 weeks for delivery.